SOUS LES TOITS DE

№ 0 0 1 3

№ 0 0 1 9

№ 0 0 1 4

№ 0 0 2 0

№ 0 0 1 5

№ 0 0 2 1

№ 0 0 1 6

№ 0 0 2 2

№ 0 0 1 7

№ 0 0 2 3

№ 0 0 1 8

№ 0 0 2 4

I & M

№ 0 0 2 5

№ 0 0 2 6

№ 0 0 2 7

№ 0 0 2 8

№ 0 0 2 9

№ 0 0 3 0

№ 0 0 3 1

№ 0 0 3 2

№ 0 0 3 3

№ 0 0 3 4

№ 0 0 3 5

№ 0 0 3 6

MAISON

PARISIAN CHIC AT HOME

Editorial Contributor
Catherine Bézard

Editorial Director
Kate Mascaro

Editor
Helen Adedotun

Translated from the French by
Philippa Hurd

Design and Typesetting
Romain Chirat – Établissements Studio

Copyediting
Penelope Isaac

Proofreading
Sam Wythe

Production
Corinne Trovarelli and Margot Jourdan

Color Separation
Quat'Coul, Paris

Printed in Spain by
Indice

Simultaneously published in French as *Sous les toits de Paris*
© Flammarion, S.A., Paris, 2018

English-language edition
© Flammarion, S.A., Paris, 2018

18 19 20   3 2 1
ISBN: 978-2-08-020367-0
Legal Deposit: 10/2018

INES DE LA FRESSANGE
MARIN MONTAGUT

MAISON
PARISIAN CHIC AT HOME

Photography by Claire Cocano
Illustrations by Marin Montagut

Flammarion

A carved eighteenth-century panel lit by a small industrial lamp, a watering can masquerading as a vase, or a hatbox upcycled into a coffee table—these are the hallmarks of a new, as yet unnamed style of interior decoration that has been adopted everywhere in Paris: from Saint-Germain-des-Prés to the Buttes Chaumont, passing through the Marais to the banks of the Seine. A blend of flea-market finds, souvenirs from foreign travels, and treasures unearthed in the family attic, this new style reveals how everything we love can coexist harmoniously.

The French poet and surrealist Paul Éluard said, "There's no such thing as chance—only encounters." And that sums up our first meeting, too. (Marin—an interior designer's assistant at the time—was perched on top of a stepladder hanging a painting when Ines walked into the room.) Very quickly, we realized that we had the same taste—in stepladders (!), but also in antiques, interiors, and fashion. After repeatedly falling in love-at-first-sight with the same items, we decided to decrypt this "neo-deco" trend that, although understated, is definitely making waves in Paris.

Taking the road less traveled, we sought out apartments or houses whose interiors are "lived in" rather than "decorated." All of the Parisians who opened their doors to us have put their heart and soul into expressing their world and embellishing the details of everyday life—and they divulged their secrets to us along the way. Their guiding principle is to combine everything: the new with the old, the sophisticated with the antiquated, the luxurious with the simple. Furniture can be stripped, distressed, or restored—as long as the result exudes charm.

In this book—by revealing inspirational ideas, highlighting an interior's essential details in watercolor illustrations, and composing mood boards that set the tone—we wanted to bring together and share all the elements that prove that a twenty-first-century style does indeed exist, reflected in interiors that are elegant, poetic, and eclectic.

We invite you to join us on our all-encompassing journey inside these homes, and to sample—without restraint—the inspiration they reveal for creating your own Parisian chic interior.

Ines de la Fressange & Marin Montagut

CONTENTS

Chez Ines

BY MARIN MONTAGUT

LE VAL DE GRÂCE DISTRICT
- PARIS 5ᵉ -

The first time you visit Ines de la Fressange's Parisian home it's like taking
a trip to the countryside—her house near the Panthéon has a garden
and is "a bit ramshackle but in a charming way." Ines has a gift for creating
an environment that's completely in her own image: cheerful, upbeat,
and unaffected. Quite simply, she collects objects and gives them a soul.
Instead of pursuing a particular style, she creates stories that
she applies to the interior.

Formerly a hotel, the house inspired her to imagine the realm of a family
boarding house with a wooden reception desk complete with a bell—
and she's pulled it off perfectly. The aroma of hot coffee makes you
want to spend the whole afternoon in the kitchen. Oversized sofas
accommodate Ines's countless friends who come to visit. Around the
extendable table, guests sit on multicolored chairs for leisurely Sunday
lunches of roast chicken. Her interiors include everything we love about
vacation homes—a constant stream of visitors, straw hats, old lamps with
silk shades, washed linen, and a riot of color. Ines loves pink because
it casts an attractive glow that is flattering for all complexions.
She is also a fan of pale green antique furniture and cream hemp fabrics.
The scent of clean linen floats through the house, evoking the comforting
memory of childhood homes. Bouquets of flowers are testament to how
much Ines is loved by the friends and family she entertains so wonderfully.
The little details do the rest: the fire is always blazing in winter
and dozens of colorful candles light up the room.

Whether it's thanks to a trip to IKEA, frenzied online shopping,
or love at first sight in the Saint-Ouen flea market, Ines snaps up
furniture and objects with an almost childlike enthusiasm.
If I were asked to draw the happiest of homes, I would draw hers.

FLIRTING WITH FASHION

For Ines, interior decoration is like dressing a woman:
it depends on structure and mood. Thanks to the
house's high ceiling, she plays with proportions
by hanging a huge portrait of Karl Marx above
a small bergère armchair. The proximity of the garden
inspired her to exhibit a collection of summer hats
in vintage store display cabinets, which have been
left in their original condition. Boaters, panamas,
and wide-brimmed straw hats evoke
that vacation feeling.

BREAK WITH CONVENTION!

Shun the showroom look at all costs.
Light pinkish-beige paint gives the impression
that the walls have been tinted by the smoke
of the wood fire. To avoid the conventional
and embrace the unexpected, a "ramshackle" style
has been created using mismatched chairs, picked up
here and there and repainted in different colors.
The bookcase is long and low—the perfect spot
for a procession of candlesticks and bud vases.

TOTALLY TEXTILE

Paintings, mirrors, and trinkets are the essence
of interior decoration, but fabrics play an equally
important role—precious materials such as damask
silks and velvets or fashionable fabrics including linen
and hemp. These raw-looking materials show off
their natural qualities and ecological virtues best
in counterpanes, cushions, and mattress toppers.
In her Paris store, Ines stocks attractive fabrics
made by hand in Africa by the Tensira brand.

LIGHT UP YOUR LIFE

If table lamps, sconces, and standard lamps are not
quite enough to create a dramatic evening ambience,
candles can provide extra softness. Set in candelabras
or individual candlesticks, they can be white, black,
or many different colors. Trudon's original approach to
making candles, with a golden inset cameo and their
palette of vintage colors, provides an eighteenth-century
charm. As each scented candle melts, it leaves behind
traces of a beautiful image on marble and glass.

PANORAMAS AND LAYERING

Sometimes it's best to invest in just one beautiful thing.
This panoramic wallpaper by Zuber & Cie called
Hindustan has been printed using 1,265 woodblocks
carved in 1807. The lavishness of the wallpaper
is kept in check thanks to the day beds composed
of a box spring and several mattress toppers.
These can be purchased ready-made or can be created
at home using interesting fabrics if you have nimble
fingers. A profusion of printed cushions provides
the finishing touch.

TABLE DECOR

Follow Ines's example: don't banish your Sunday-best tableware to the cupboard while you use only old basics every day. Handmade artisan ceramics and pottery are skillfully made and feel so much nicer—they should be enjoyed time and again. Enameled dishes and casseroles also have an old-fashioned appeal that works well in kitchens. White, gold, and pastel items bring a magical touch to the table, starting at breakfast, especially when they coordinate with the color of the tablecloth.

I SING THE BODY ELECTRIC

Of course, stainless steel always shines in minimalist
kitchens. But if your kitchen is a bit more rustic,
household appliances can be used to add a welcome
splash of color. These days, many electric mixers, scales,
and slow cookers come in almost every hue imaginable.
For Ines, a touch of pink on the countertop makes
the kitchen much more attractive. And small wooden
crates make ideal containers for fruit and vegetables.

PUT A LABEL ON IT

As a model and fashion designer, Ines needs no lessons in storing clothes and accessories. The walk-in wardrobe in a small room adjoining the bathroom consists of simple shelves on which clothes are stacked by type. Small, everyday items are collected in transparent boxes made by Muji, while the contents of large cardboard boxes are hand-labeled. On the wardrobe doors, a jumble of sweet Post-it notes inject some poetry into the room.

STACKING AND HANGING

The powder-pink and pale green ambience makes you want to spend rainy days in bed, reading or working. Books are piled up in a stack on the floor or on a narrow table. The fireplace, with its surround of beautiful tiles, houses a pyramid of colorful trunks and suitcases. A gingham basket offers a cheerful contrast to the dominant color palette. The Empire-style overmantel is flanked by two twentieth-century floral sconces in gilded brass—with a little chain suspended between them to complete the look.

PANTONE PINK AND SCOUBIDOUS

To find your perfect pink, the Pantone color chart
is a must—an indispensable tool when you're working
with color. The distressed paintwork on a vintage
kitchen sideboard can be retained, as long as the
stepladder and wooden stool are given a fresh coat
of paint for contrast. For those who enjoy weaving—
or just looking at pretty colors—scoubidou plastic
threads are displayed on reels or in baskets.

GET THE LOOK

Fig. 1

Use polychrome and terra-cotta faience tiles hailing from the early twentieth century, or Delft tiles which are older.

Fig. 2

These tiny wire or stainless-steel shelves can be hung in hidden corners around the house.

Fig. 3

Beautiful antique linen embroidered with initials in elegant red stitching can be used to make cushion covers.

Fig. 4

Buly pomade comes in an attractively illustrated tube and is perfect for moisturizing hands and feet as it's made with shea butter, beeswax, and sesame oil.

Fig. 5

Ideal for small DIY jobs or reaching high shelves, a vintage wooden stepladder can be repainted any way you like.

Fig. 6

Moroccan stools made of wood and straw are child-size, but also work as footstools for grown-ups.

Fig. 7

Collect coffee pots in charming floral patterns; used as vases, they make bouquets look great.

Fig. 8

Ines adores all kinds of baskets, particularly small ones made of raffia that are great for storing socks, hair accessories, and makeup.

Fig. 9

Trawl flea markets for old bottles in slender shapes; they make perfect containers for single cut flowers.

"I love pink when it casts a pretty, flattering light, but I also like galvanized metal, anything copper, washed linen and, above all, lime-washed walls."

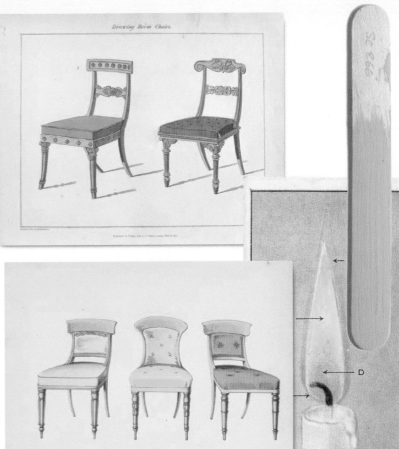

"I don't think you should impose your own 'style' on a house, but instead you should imagine its history and adapt the decor to suit the story. It's like choosing the right clothes for a woman!"

Karl Marx.

Chez Marin

BY INES DE LA FRESSANGE

LA FOLIE-MÉRICOURT DISTRICT
- PARIS 11ᵉ -

Stepping into Marin Montagut's home is like receiving a gift—it's a happy, timeless moment. Listening to the falling rain, enjoying the beautiful view of the zinc rooftops, hearing the creaks of the wooden floorboards—and his favorite music—and examining each of the many objects in his apartment: before long, you'll want to move in! It's no surprise that this designer's interiors resemble his watercolors—cheerful, colorful, poetic, and exotic. A modern globe-trotter, Marin collaborates with brands in both the fashion and interior design worlds, but he has more than one string to his bow: he makes videos, draws, paints, writes, and illustrates guidebooks on the *art de vivre* of cities and regions, including the charming *Bonjour City Map-Guides* series.

A savvy aesthete, Marin is as discreet as the dandies of times past, and he has an innate feeling for beautiful things that he expresses in a modest way. He may love megacities, but he chose his neighborhood for its village-like atmosphere—small boutiques, food stores, and the combination of the working-class Belleville district and the more bourgeois Canal Saint-Martin—and especially for the old Parisian charm of the eleventh arrondissement. Inspired by his visits to flea markets around the world and the antiques markets of his beloved Normandy, he has completely revamped his apartment of 516 square feet (48 m²) to surround himself with his treasures so that he can enjoy them at all times. He had the kitchen wall demolished to bring light in through a glass partition, relaid his floor with hexagonal red terra-cotta tiles in the style of bygone maid's quarters, and removed the false parquet to reveal the original oak floor. Marin then gave full rein to his artistic instincts, without waiting for a timeworn patina to showcase all his treasures.

№ 28

CREATING SCENES

Against a backdrop of white and "English green"
walls (paints by Ressource), Marin creates his tableaux.
An old workbench showcases a cabinet of curiosities.
The palm lamp, inspired by Maison Jansen designs,
sits next to column sculptures and a glass dome in
which a hermit crab slumbers for all eternity.
The wrought-iron console table boasts a rare find:
a Pierre Giraudon resin and coral lamp, sourced
in Marseille. Everywhere, candles are grouped
together to form little "families."

Visions in Watercolor

In his canvas fisherman's bag, Marin's
watercolor box is always within reach,
so he can pull it out to sketch details
of a landscape or a trinket.
His passion for art has encouraged
him to collect old drawing
boards and painters'
palettes—they're
made of ordinary
wood but each
tells a story.
Palettes belonging
to famous artists may
be found only in museums, but
those used by amateurs can be picked up
at garage sales. They're little works of art
in themselves that look attractive propped
up on the floor.

A COZY BOUDOIR

Covered with Indian fabrics and cushions that
coordinate with the kilim carpet, the chaise longue
is placed under the window facing a custom-made
mirror, which reflects the light from roofs and sky.
Under another palm lamp, a detail reproduction from
Michelangelo's Sistine Chapel ceiling sits in a carved
wooden frame. A papier-mâché cachepot against
the wall adds a flash of color. Marin picked up
the plaster head of Aphrodite when he was in Kyoto
for an exhibition of his watercolors.

IT'S ALL IN THE DETAIL

In a barn on a farm in Normandy, Marin came across two perfectly proportioned old doors that add inimitable character. The stripped wood kitchen cabinets from IKEA gain a hint of luxury when paired with pink Moroccan *zellige* tiles by Emery. Brushes brought back by Marin from each of his trips are hung on the tiles under the watchful gaze of a ceramic dog carafe—an old-fashioned touch that transforms everything. The folding, circular vineyard table painted in black showcases a teapot and vase by Astier de Villatte.

LIKE A MOTH TO A FLAME

Setting up a miniature natural history museum on an old sideboard always sparks the imagination. An entomology collection can be created from ready-made glass cases, or by making a personal selection from the many varieties and colors of butterflies to be found in the huge drawers at natural history suppliers such as Deyrolle—a Parisian cabinet of curiosities and shop specialized in taxidermy, entomology, and natural sciences. Old marbled notebooks are stacked around a sparkling crystal sulfur paperweight, which may soon be the inspiration for a new collection.

GET THE LOOK

Fig. 1

Fashionable during the Second Empire, a red gorgonian coral mounted on a turned wooden plinth can kick-start your cabinet of curiosities.

Fig. 2

Found languishing in an antiques store in Granville, Normandy, this early 1950s plate is typical of the thousands of designs produced by Piero Fornasetti.

Fig. 3

This religious statue made of wood with glass eyes was brought back from a trip to Portugal.

Fig. 4

Collecting vintage pharmacy bottles, for either use or decoration, is the ultimate pleasure—or perhaps therapy— for hypochondriacs.

Fig. 5

As a child, all you had to do was close your eyes, spin the globe, and stop it with your finger to select the trip of your dreams.

Fig. 6

Mini dustpan-and-brush sets, often made as children's toys, were picked up at flea markets while traveling.

Fig. 7

This slipware fish jug, a typical Portuguese design, was bought at A Vida Portuguesa in Lisbon.

Fig. 8

A little-known portrait of Marie Antoinette has been transformed into a royal candle by Trudon.

Fig. 9

The iconic lavender Eau de Cologne Lavanda, in the Musgo Real shaving collection, was created in Porto in the 1930s by Claus Porto.

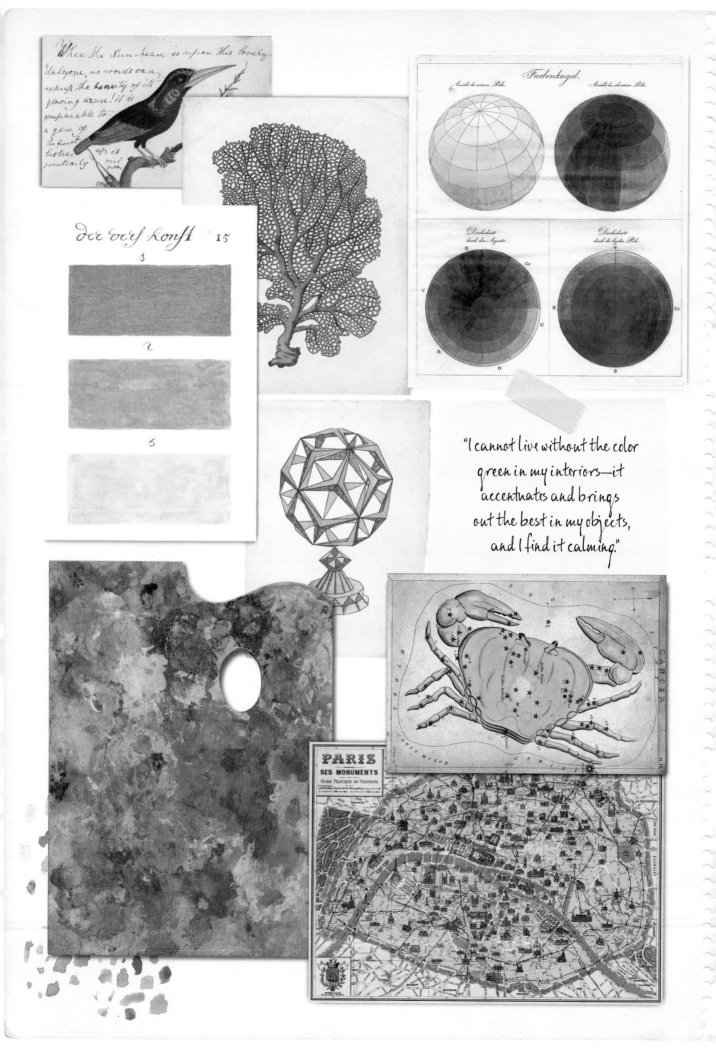

When the Sun-beam is upon this lovely Halcyone, no words can express the beauty of its glowing azure! it is comparable to a gem of the finest turbies. It is peculiarly our own...

der verf kunst 15

1

2

3

Farbenkugel.

"I cannot live without the color green in my interiors—it accentuates and brings out the best in my objects, and I find it calming."

PARIS
SES MONUMENTS
GUIDE PRATIQUE DU VISITEUR

"I love building little tableaux that tell a story. Being surrounded by my objects is a daily source of inspiration in my work."

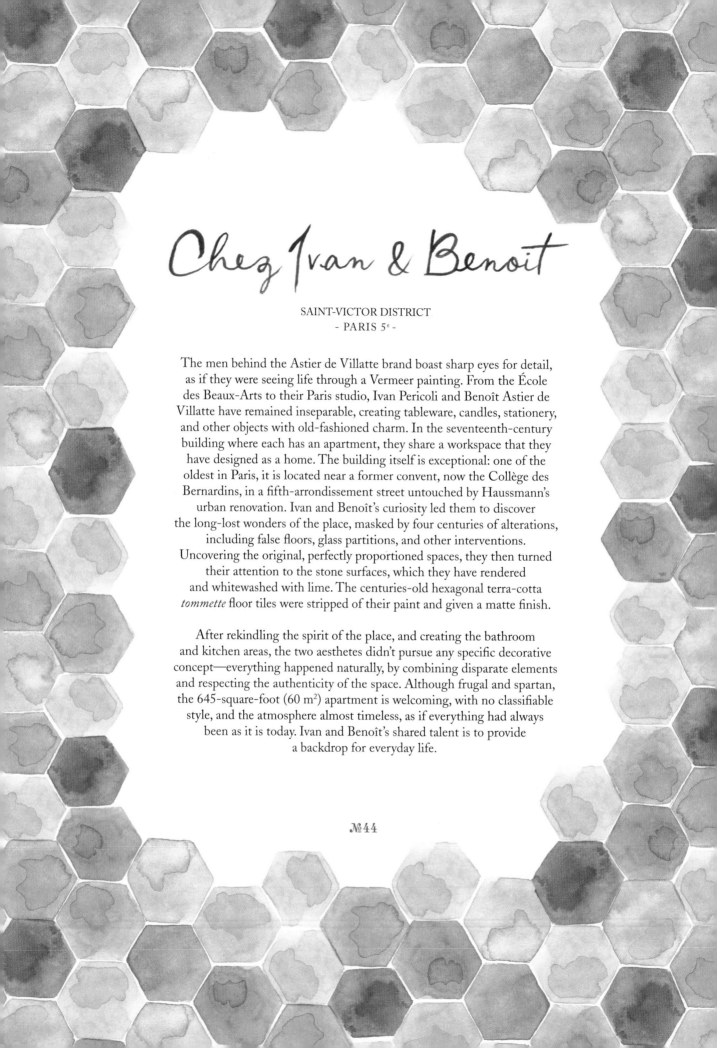

Chez Ivan & Benoît

The men behind the Astier de Villatte brand boast sharp eyes for detail, as if they were seeing life through a Vermeer painting. From the École des Beaux-Arts to their Paris studio, Ivan Pericoli and Benoît Astier de Villatte have remained inseparable, creating tableware, candles, stationery, and other objects with old-fashioned charm. In the seventeenth-century building where each has an apartment, they share a workspace that they have designed as a home. The building itself is exceptional: one of the oldest in Paris, it is located near a former convent, now the Collège des Bernardins, in a fifth-arrondissement street untouched by Haussmann's urban renovation. Ivan and Benoît's curiosity led them to discover the long-lost wonders of the place, masked by four centuries of alterations, including false floors, glass partitions, and other interventions. Uncovering the original, perfectly proportioned spaces, they then turned their attention to the stone surfaces, which they have rendered and whitewashed with lime. The centuries-old hexagonal terra-cotta *tommette* floor tiles were stripped of their paint and given a matte finish.

After rekindling the spirit of the place, and creating the bathroom and kitchen areas, the two aesthetes didn't pursue any specific decorative concept—everything happened naturally, by combining disparate elements and respecting the authenticity of the space. Although frugal and spartan, the 645-square-foot (60 m²) apartment is welcoming, with no classifiable style, and the atmosphere almost timeless, as if everything had always been as it is today. Ivan and Benoît's shared talent is to provide a backdrop for everyday life.

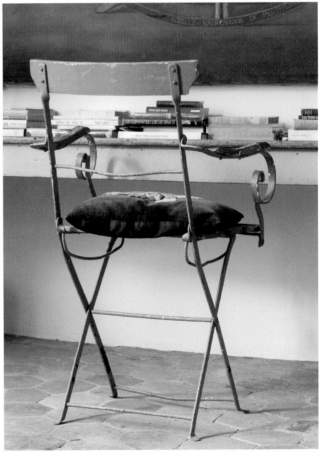

SPARTAN ELEGANCE

Why not set aside functionality and focus solely
on creating a tableau? Objects or furniture found
at flea markets do not have to be beautiful; when they
are showcased, they reveal their true nature and form
a harmonious, highly pictorial ensemble. The Tibetan
tiger carpet from the Liberty store in London evokes
memories of expeditions and adds an exotic flavor.

TURN ON THE CHARM

Contrary to popular belief, it's actually quite easy to pick up antique finds at affordable prices. A delicate Second Empire-style inlaid chair or gueridon table provide touches of elegance. An improvised chaise longue— composed simply of a box spring, a mattress, a beautiful canvas bedspread, and Tibetan tapestry cushions—is enough to create an intimate corner alongside an intriguing collection of trinkets.

IT'S ALL ABOUT SPACE

One fundamental rule says that the smaller the space,
the more you should fill it; the larger it is, the more it
needs clean lines. The pink sofa and the elongated table
made from an old door balanced on trestles were chosen
to create an impression of expansiveness. The mirror
and the large painting by Benoît's father emphasize
this feeling of space. The grand sofas contrast with
the delicate chairs, including one salvaged from
a vintage set of garden furniture.

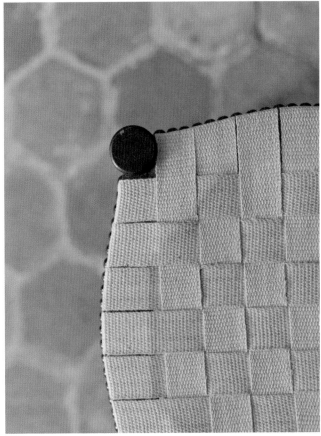

Create Still Lifes

Turn painterly subjects such as books, objects, and flowers into compositions ready to be sketched by an artist: for example, an edition of works by Marcel Proust dating from the 1950s, a vase, a dish, and an Astier de Villatte marbleized teapot. Stack books on the table (instead of on shelves) to make them more inviting to read. Sober lighting suspends the decorative elements in a dusky atmosphere that accentuates the spatial volume.

GET THE LOOK

Fig. 1

A marbleized teapot, created in collaboration with New York designer John Derian.

Fig. 2

A salad bowl from the Corail Bleu collection of Astier de Villatte ceramics.

Fig. 3

Astier de Villatte's iconic notebooks sport trompe-l'œil floor-tile patterns borrowed from the decorative arts of bygone times.

Fig. 4

Forage for vintage handmade tapestry fabrics to make imaginative cushion covers.

Fig. 5

Typically found in seventeenth-century Paris, the brick-red color of the *tommette* floor tiles has faded, creating an attractive, timeworn look.

Fig. 6

A vintage pendant lamp with its white ceramic, tulip-shaped lampshade casts a lovely subdued light.

Fig. 7

Salt and pepper shakers, sugar bowl, or mustard pot—all sorts of kitsch porcelain can be combined with other finds to great effect.

Fig. 8

Create decorative finishing touches with flowers scattered around in jugs, old candleholders, or bottles.

Fig. 9

A large velvet-covered imitation Louis XV-style chair is inexpensive but very comfortable.

MOUCHOIR CASE.—See Description.
By June 1852.
Design—Geometric

"We wanted to remain as true
as possible to the authenticity
of the place, so we've tried to create
a natural, unpretentious mixture,
as if the apartment had always
been decorated like this, without
knowing by whom or when. A kind
of suspended, timeless atmosphere—
beyond style, you might say."

BIBLIOTECA NAZ.
Vittorio Emanuele III
113
O
27
NAPOLI

№ 1
№ 2
№ 3
№ 4
№ 5
№ 6

"The walls had been crudely covered over by the previous tenants—but underneath we found stone masonry that we have whitewashed with lime."

"The period architects knew how to create spaces with perfect dimensions. We just had to go back to the original site plan to reveal the classic beauty of the place, which recalls Vermeer's paintings of interiors."

Chez Ariane

AUTEUIL DISTRICT
- PARIS 16ᵉ -

A broad palette of green tones brings the great outdoors into the interior of this apartment belonging to Ariane Dalle, artistic director of prestigious fabric brands Manuel Canovas and Larsen, who was inspired by happy childhood memories of Provençal landscapes.

A sense of nature pervades the artfully displayed items in this 861-square-foot (80 m²) space, which has been converted into three rooms, with curved windows and an original kitchen. Ariane's personality shines through in the recurring themes, skillful arrangements, and emotive collections, all infused with a 1920s vibe. An avid collector of random items from her travels in India and elsewhere in Asia or picked up at flea markets and antiques fairs from New York to Paris, Ariane liberates them from their original use, calling their past a "mysterious skein that weaves us together." These eclectic tendencies inspired her to create this bohemian space in Paris's otherwise rather conventional sixteenth arrondissement.

The patina of vintage, utilitarian furniture instills a warm atmosphere and a unique character, while wood, stoneware, and glass exude a classical beauty. Fabrics become a source of inspiration: drapes made from dhoti fabric (lengths of white cotton traditionally worn by South Asian men), cushions covered with jute (as used in the American West to make flour sacks), and a Miao bedspread from the Yunnan region of China weave their own tales.

Ariane escapes from the gray of Paris and dreams of the South of France by planning her next purchase: a table lamp by Roger Capron, the famous ceramicist based in Vallauris on the French Riviera.

HISTORY IN THE MAKING

Create successful harmonies by filling the space
to make proportions seem larger. Placed in the corner
and piled high with cushions, a chaise longue
is a luxurious alternative to the traditional sofa.
Hanging above the fireplace, which is covered with a
range of different objects, the mirror creates multiple
perspectives and reflections. The vintage kitchen sideboard
showcases some beautiful finds, such as the demijohn
bottles named for Queen Jeanne; she had containers
like these made in Provence when she was exiled
from her home kingdom of Naples.

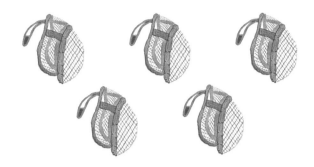

CREATE DEPTH

Showcase your collection of tiny treasures by painting the wall a dark color to create depth and volume. The graphic quality of modern lettering is complemented by the classic typography of the neatly stacked old tins and cans. A vintage lamp provides eye-catching illumination. The mesh fencing masks—almost transparent and perfectly designed—are mounted on the wall like trophies above randomly arranged numbered signs.

BROUGHT TO BOOK

Who needs a bookcase to store reading material?
On their own, books can easily furnish a room, if you
make a feature of the colors on their covers and spines.
Piling them high creates a cozy atmosphere, and there are
many ways of doing this: arrange them on a military trunk
found in the cellar or bought in an army surplus store;
layer them to make an ingenious pyramid on the floor,
or stack them on a table, some vertically,
some horizontally.

THE SPIRIT OF REINVENTION

Try grouping lots of different items by type—objects, tools, or advertising signage—before displaying them on a piece of furniture or hanging them on a wall. Liberating vintage pieces from their original use is another way to breathe new life into them: an old thermos flask morphs into a vase, and a birdcage houses a collection of succulents, which purify the air and calm the mind.

MORE IS MORE

Playing with a space by using lots of mirrors
is the secret to creating a vibrant interior.
Mirrors perfectly reflect paintings, plants,
or furniture, and accentuate lighting effects.
Go green and invent landscapes using demijohns,
with or without their wicker covers. And to create
the illusion of a huge space, stack up chests
and old-fashioned wooden crates, which also
provide useful storage.

SET THE STAGE

For a decorative style to look natural, it takes more than improvisation: it's about mastering materials, colors, and volumes. In contrast to the dominant green hues of the apartment, black and white are used to create a kitchen setting that showcases pottery, ceramics, and even license plates. Domestic items from times gone by lend themselves to all kinds of upcycling: an old *garde-manger* food safe becomes the perfect home for pristine breakfast crockery, a collection of spice jars, or even small plants.

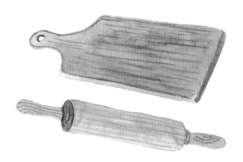

HOMESPUN CHARM

Anything handmade or handcrafted is a welcome addition to the charm of an interior. The creamy harmony of a collection of ceramic bottles, carafes, or white containers can be both useful and decorative when sporting a few dried flower and grass stems. Take your imagination back to the drawing board with wooden items that blend harmoniously with the decor: make a collection of simple chopping boards or rolling pins.

A6062 VERMONT 53

NH-53 **AO248**

7333 **1963**

Timeworn and Timeless

Create an element of surprise by adding retro nooks and corners—an art that can be cultivated by recycling, upcycling, and frequent visits to flea markets. Aim for perfection by stocking bookshelves with books all from the same period, or books with elegantly matching covers. Vintage volumes with well-thumbed, yellowing pages provide a decorative element, supplemented by old license plates, measuring weights, and Mason jars. Whether opaque or transparent, these jars tell their own story. These molded glass containers with screw-on lids were invented in the late nineteenth century by John Landis Mason, revolutionizing the preservation of food at home.

A SECRET CHAMBER

Imagine each room as a secret chamber where
the most antiquated and precious things cluster
together in natural groups. A lovingly assembled
mixture of bamboo-framed mirrors, seashells, glass
butterfly cases, stoneware pots, and wicker containers
creates a collection to rival a cabinet of curiosities.
Favorite pieces are showcased on shelves made from
a fisherman's crate or are suspended from a louvered
shutter whose paint has been gently stripped away
to reveal traces of its past.

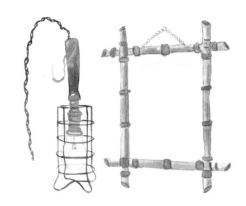

SHINE A LIGHT

Alongside natural sunlight, artificial
illumination sculpts, conceals, and reveals space
in an almost cinematic play of light and shade.
Vary the intensity to infuse objects with color and
highlight their shapes. Multiply light sources—both
by day and by night—to create different ambiences.
An inspection lamp, the vestige of a construction site,
casts its beam across the walls and ceiling, drawing
beautiful arabesques as it moves.

GET THE LOOK

Fig. 1

Create a bohemian vibe
with this African basket, woven
with eye-catching patterns
and hung on the wall.

Fig. 2

A small wicker picnic basket
can be recycled to provide
storage.

Fig. 3

The writing's on the wall with
these vintage signage letters.

Fig. 4

A vintage birdcage makes
a charming home for
plants or a table lamp.

Fig. 5

Hang a group of
barbers' mirrors on the wall
to create different perspectives
and light effects.

Fig. 6

Rugs and throws collected
on your travels can be draped
casually over chairs.

Fig. 7

Start a new collection inspired
by this wooden stamp brought
back from India.

Fig. 8

An old-fashioned lunch pail
turns utility into decoration.

Fig. 9

Brightly colored baskets made
of wicker or rush provide storage
and look especially pretty.

"I don't like ostentation. For me, simplicity is everything—beauty wrought by time, raw materials, the patina of things. As I spent my childhood in the countryside of Provence, I need the color green to remind me of nature amid this urban grayness!"

SMALL COPPER BUTTERFLY

BASKET FOR MERCHANDISE.

ABC

"I like to be eclectic, searching flea markets for collections of simple, everyday objects, whose time-worn appearance reveals their beauty."

Chez Zoé

VIVIENNE DISTRICT
- PARIS 2ᵉ -

Zoé de Las Cases and her partner are graphic designers, illustrators,
and interior designers who found their little nest perched above the clouds
on the rooftops of Paris. It lies at the end of Rue Montmartre, close
to the Grands-Boulevards metro station. With childhood nostalgia,
Zoé uses colored pencils for her illustrations of clothing, decorative
objects, branding sketches, and interior plans.

Zoé, Benjamin, Olya (five), and Sacha (three), plus Napoléon the dog,
were catapulted from a loft apartment located on the ground floor
of a seventeenth-arrondissement building into a duplex with a terrace
in the second arrondissement that had to be completely renovated.
Parisians are not afraid of big projects, especially when they fall in love
with the view, the neighborhood, the light—and the chance to have a
rustic fireplace. Since her childhood holidays in Aubrac—a small village
on a windswept plateau straddling the Aveyron, Cantal, and Lozère
departments in central and southern France—Zoé has never lost her love
of wild things. Tree branches, ladders, and tabletops, grayed by the passage
of time, remind her of the freedom of wide-open spaces. A breath of fresh
air and a sense of profusion inhabit this all-white apartment. The light
caresses her carefully selected objects and the comfortable curves
of the architecture. Elegant materials take precedence over any
compulsion to be decorative. Vintage and designer pieces quietly enjoy
each other's company. In her rooftop aerie, Zoé has succeeded
in creating a charming space for relaxation and pleasure.

№ 76

CHILL-OUT CHIMNEY

Beneath the white-painted original beams, the Jieldé lamp
designed by Jean-Louis Domecq in 1950 harmonizes
timelessly with the Apple iMac, as the styles chime
and echo across the decades. The presence of the bespoke
black fireplace is betrayed only by a log-filled rattan
basket. As a fashionable addition, old planks serve
as a coffee table, and the white sofa blends seamlessly
with the floor. Pristine white or powder-pink objects
and furniture create a serene atmosphere.

GOOD FENCES MAKE
GOOD NEIGHBORS

Even if the building opposite overlooks your apartment,
in Paris you can be sure that no one is peering in.
Nevertheless, a terrace should be regarded as an
independent living and entertaining space. Adding
a protective wooden screen means you can grow ivy or
clematis along it to create a secret place high above the
city. Bistro chairs, stools, and wooden benches—it takes
just a few items to create a hint of luxury. The cushions
covered with ethnic fabrics by Tensira evoke happy
trips to far-flung places.

SIMPLE BEAUTY

Trust your deepest convictions when designing spaces,
as this will ensure they are both natural and surprising.
Above the kitchen counter, traditional iron pendant lamps
are suspended from a branch cut from a tree in Normandy,
while pickle-jar lights hang above the table. The whiteness
of both the hob and oven adds depth. Sawed from an old
workbench covered with drops of paint, Zoé's table
is surrounded by mismatched bistro chairs;
it dominates the living room.

FUNCTIONAL DELICACY

From the school of eco-design, a wooden lamp by Wood & Scrap satisfies a desire for a more equitable world. In pursuit of this ideal, cables and plugs are hidden inside a toy truck by Serendipity. Illustrations culled from herbaria provide a hymn to nature when hung in groups. A bespoke glass partition separates the bedroom from the bathroom. Old tiles are propped up like pictures, while a Muji cuckoo clock chimes in with a contemporary note.

BATHTIME

Recalling Greek vacations, the shelves and niches have
been carved into the wall. Pretty beauty products by
Buly are arranged so they are easily accessible. A natural
stone sink serves as a hand basin, whose pure lines are
highlighted by black faucets. The multitude of mirrors
on the wall makes it easy to see the world from all angles.
No ecologically unfriendly towel heaters here—just a
simple ladder for drying towels.

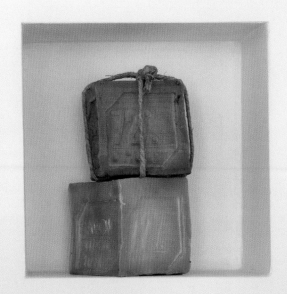

TENDER MOMENTS

The children have their own dedicated space where old-school gender hues are still in service, with pink for a girl and blue for a boy, and a garden chair to separate the two. The child-sized furniture, designed by Zoé to be both fun and decorative, echoes the spirit of the children's own washbasin, which they reach by climbing up a set of steps, painted a sunflower yellow for visual impact.

GET THE LOOK

Fig. 1

Purloined from seventeenth-century natural history cabinets, dried plant specimens have a poetry all their own. Look out for them in flea markets or make them yourself at home.

Fig. 2

Used when picnicking at the Château de Versailles or on special outings, these water bottles are decorative repositories of happy memories.

Fig. 3

Designed by Mullca in the 1950s, this little chair used to be a common sight in schools and civic centers—now it's a lucky find for collectors!

Fig. 4

Instead of the usual brushed steel or shiny stainless-steel faucets, why not try gold to contrast with the simplicity of a rough stone washbasin.

Fig. 5

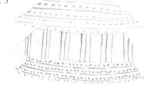

Use mattress toppers and African-made cushions by Tensira to create cozy corners on the terrace.

Fig. 6

A single flower is all it takes: buds arranged in pharmacy bottles produce a charming effect.

Fig. 7

Out with harsh white lighting and in with filament bulbs that lighten the atmosphere with a warm, mellow glow.

Fig. 8

Handmade wooden toys are just as much fun for parents as for kids. Pepper them throughout the home as a reminder of the joys of childhood.

Fig. 9

Designed to produce carbonated liquids and add fizz to alcoholic drinks, soda siphons are obsolete today—which makes them all the more collectible.

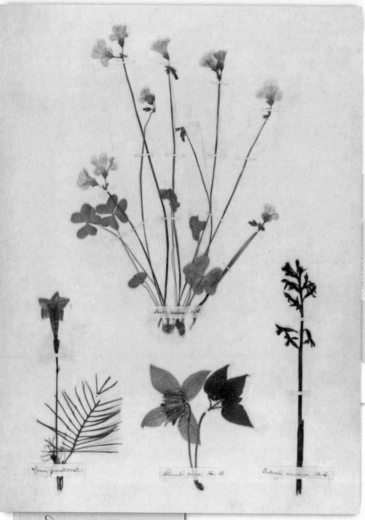

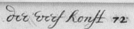

der Verf Kunst **72**

"I like simple, natural
things, and I have my own
style of combining old pieces
with contemporary design.
I like evoking the
countryside in the city and
the city in the country."

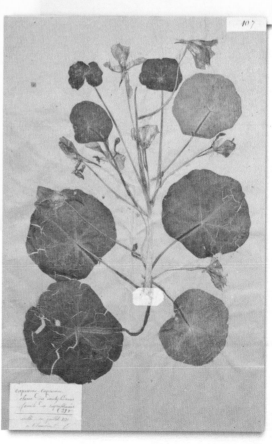

107

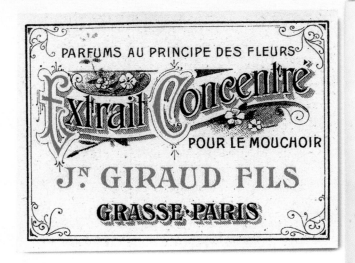

PARFUMS AU PRINCIPE DES FLEURS
Extrait Concentré
POUR LE MOUCHOIR
Jn GIRAUD FILS
GRASSE·PARIS

"My sources of inspiration for our apartment are nature, light, and poetry."

— PAPAVERACEÆ —

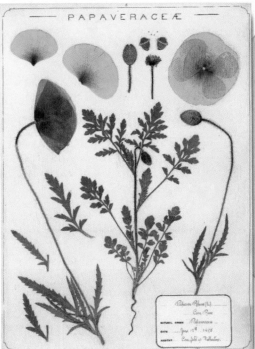

EVERYBODY LIKES
TO
WASH WITH
GOOD WILL SOAP

Chez Daniel

LES ARCHIVES DISTRICT

- PARIS 3ᵉ -

There's not much that Daniel Rozensztroch doesn't know about antique hunting. He never tires of scouring secondhand stores, garage sales, flea markets, hardware stores, and bazaars the world over. The artistic director of the Parisian concept store Merci, Daniel is a compulsive connoisseur of everything that makes everyday life more beautiful. Curiosity has sharpened his judgment about what can become beautiful, once placed in the right setting. And—*merci!*—that's exactly what his passions and instincts achieve at Merci.

When searching for a new apartment, Daniel came across a town house built by Gustave Eiffel in 1870 for a toy manufacturer on Rue de Turenne. He acquired an open-plan space of 1,076 square feet (100 m²), set amid a French-style garden, whose industrial architecture enabled him to create an uninterrupted loft apartment with areas and functions that are nevertheless well defined. He designed it with his architect friend Valérie Mazérat, both of them fans of the color black. Pride of place here might be given to the spoon, an object to which Daniel has dedicated a book, but this style globe-trotter has never parted ways with his copy of Michelangelo's Moses, a sculpture that he inherited from his grandparents. It is, without a doubt, his primary source of inspiration. Raw materials take precedence, and Daniel's passion for twisted wire creates unusual figures that bring life to this perfectly designed space. Nothing has been thrown away and everything has been assembled—almost itemized—to reveal its essence: the happiness derived from living and entertaining in a unique environment, completely devoted to beauty.

BLACK IS BLACK

Black on black or white on white—the perfectly monochromatic palette is enhanced by a touch of red from an industrial-style faucet. Glassware and earthenware form a balanced composition in which graphic simplicity outweighs cost—and that's what counts. Spaces are divided up using metal or wooden furniture of different shapes and sizes. The back of one piece of furniture has been transformed into a workbench bulletin board, creating a vertical cabinet of treasured curiosities accumulated over time as souvenirs or flea-market finds.

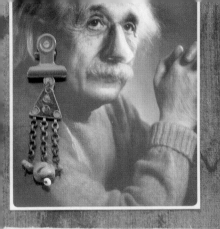

FILETS de HARENGS SAURS
AU NATUREL

BOULOGNE·SUR·MER

NET
200 Grs

AUX DEUX AMIS

R R R

R

24

LUMIÈRE

R

R

merci

grazie

merci

LES PINCES

FFA

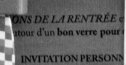
...ONS DE LA RENTRÉE e...
...vons-... ...tour d'un bon verre pour...

INVITATION PERSONN...

mat...
...the right s...

Samedi 6 septembr...
de 19 à 22 heures...

La lutte
CONTINUE

...RADERIE DE LA MODE
...ON AIDES AU PROFIT DE LA LUTTE CONTRE LE SIDA...
...IMANCHE 11 DÉCEMBRE 2016   Aides
...raderiedelamode.aides.org

merci sera ouvert exceptionnellement le dimanch...

merci
111 boulevard beaumarchais 75003 Paris...
www.merci-merci.com

ALPHABETICAL ORDER

In the sunny glow of Isamu Noguchi's L8 Akari
light, oil jugs and carafes stand out against the black
backdrop. The metal shelves of the bookcase lend
structure to the space. Letters from vintage signs evoke
mysterious messages. White-painted trestles support
a zinc tabletop. Above the table surrounded
by Tolix chairs, In the Tube hanging lamps
(by Dominique Perrault and Gaëlle Lauriot-Prévost
for DCW) illuminate the eclecticism
and timelessness of the space.

DESIGN CLASSICS

In the living room (see page 101) the Aalto vase
and Eero Saarinen gueridon table sit side by side with
an African stool atop a checkerboard-pattern rug.
The Mantis BS3 lamp by Schottlander spars with
Paola Navone's Ghost sofa, while ethnic wooden
tableware is lined up on a slab of carved stone. A note
of stylistic independence is struck in the bedroom-cum-
dressing room, where storage informs the decor with
an open wardrobe, matching hangers, American pool
baskets, and a 1950s medicine cabinet.

GET THE LOOK

Fig. 1

Trips to Japan, the United States, and Africa have shaped an eclectic taste that encompasses everything from rare finds to a pack of sponges.

Fig. 2

Made in Provence, jugs and carafes in glazed terra-cotta are perfect containers for water, wine, or olive oil.

Fig. 3

Featuring striking prints and encrusted with beads, a collection of African bracelets and cuffs is wonderfully sculptural.

Fig. 4

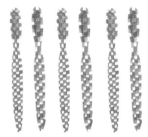

If Philippe Starck's toothbrush can be exhibited at the Centre Pompidou, why not start your own collection of toothbrushes picked up around the globe?

Fig. 5

Works of art in and of themselves, with their eye-catching spines, covers, and of course their contents, art books are striking objects when displayed in number.

Fig. 6

Sculpted from mother-of-pearl or carved from a twig, these spoons are among the treasures documented by Daniel Rozensztroch in his book *Spoon* (Pointed Leaf Press).

Fig. 7

Any everyday object made by hand, such as this wooden kitchen brush, can become a decorative piece.

Fig. 8

Whether it's eighteenth-century tableware or one-of-a-kind nineteenth-century glassware, it's all highly collectible but should also be used without fear of breakages.

Fig. 9

Magnets are perfect for affixing your wonderful finds to metal partitions without having to drill holes.

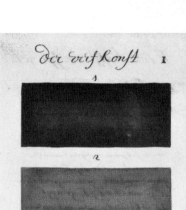

Der Brief Kunst I

OGDEN'S CIGARETTES

BEND CORNERS A & B
PUSH POINT D THROUGH
BUTTONHOLE AS FAR
AS C, THEN OPEN OUT
CORNERS A & B.

BEND CARD HERE
WHEN USED FOR HAT.

CLUB COLOUR
BADGE,
FOR BUTTONHOLE
OR HAT.

REG.º 530,973.
D

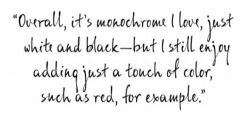

THE
ANOINTING
SPOON

CORONATION 1911.

NOT FOR PUBLICATION   FILE COPY

FILE COPY

FILE COPY

"Overall, it's monochrome I love, just white and black—but I still enjoy adding just a touch of color, such as red, for example."

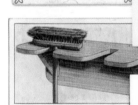

THE CORONATION SPOON

R R R
R R R

THE METROPOLITAN MUSEUM
OF ART

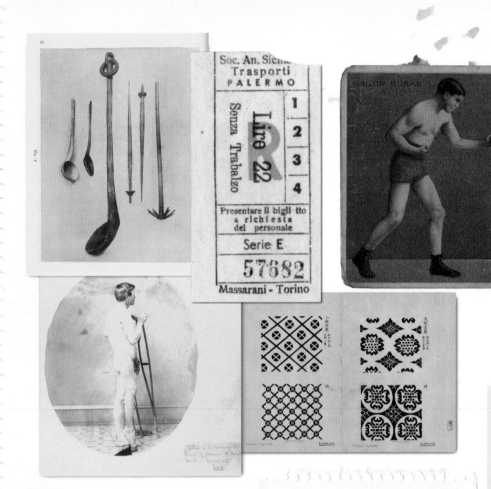

Soc. An. Sicula
Trasporti
PALERMO

Lire 22
Senza Trabalzo

1
2
3
4

Presentare il biglietto
a richiesta
del personale

Serie E

57682

Massarani - Torino

SAILOR BURKE

H.M.S. INVINCIBLE

"I don't like the idea of 'interior decoration.' I have very eclectic tastes, probably as a result of my trips to the United States as well as to Japan and Africa."

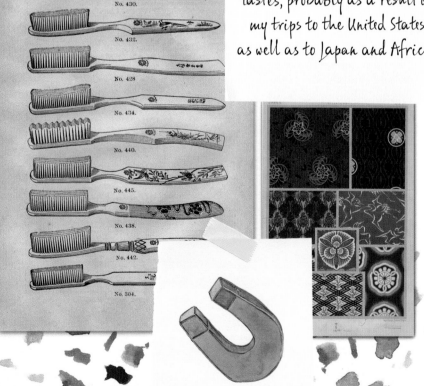

No. 430.
No. 432.
No. 428.
No. 434.
No. 440.
No. 445.
No. 438.
No. 442.
No. 304.

Chez Morgane

Morgane Sézalory, the creator of Sézane.com (France's leading online clothing brand), draws inspiration for her collections from a scrap of silk, a sketch, a space, or small, meaningful finds—and the same goes for her home. In both her professional and private life, Morgane follows her instincts.

As she searched for an oasis in pink and green, Morgane's dream came true when she discovered this 1,883-square-foot (175 m²) apartment in a beautiful eighteenth-century building in the heart of Saint-Germain-des-Prés. To her delight, the view—overlooking another beautiful building—was straight out of a movie. With its tall ceilings and historical curved walls, the apartment was just a shell, which Morgane redesigned as two separate living spaces: one for her and her husband, and another for their two children. In a bid to create harmony between structure and lifestyle, furniture and objects blend naturally into an almost organic composition. Flea-market finds, family photos, and artists' prints are placed alongside Persian rugs, all evoking happy memories; they come together, contrast, and become virtually indistinguishable. A pastel color palette is their common denominator, and these elements, informally displayed, are a feast for both the eye and the family's memories. From Lieutenant P. Castets's hand-lettered footlockers, which have accompanied Morgane since her teens, to the large mirror above the sofa or the India Mahdavi lamp (a gift from her husband), the decor conveys the spirit of the place and the people who live there.

TRADITION AND MODERNITY

Knocking down the top half of a wall to create
an expanse of glass creates striking new perspectives
and brings life and light to the interior. The furniture
is arranged along the length of this space to promote
a feeling of expansiveness. Slate gray creates depth,
while objects are moved around according to mood,
so that nothing remains fixed in place. Engravings and
paintings are propped up casually against the wall.

COLOR MAKES A HOME

The neutral walls and objects inspire a sense of freshness and freedom. White serves as a backdrop to all the other colors that sculpt the decor. The series of pendant lamps produces a beautiful halo of light. Set around a simple black wooden table, the 1950s chairs are upholstered in velvet, while the gilded brass of their legs is echoed in the cutlery. The kitchen work surface becomes a miniature altar where favorite objects are given pride of place. Everything is meticulously chosen, down to the last detail.

SOFT FOCUS

Intended to be a haven of "love, freedom, calm, and peace," the bedroom is a special place. The masonry headboard can accommodate paintings, souvenirs, or candles. The mirror enlarges the space, reflecting beloved objects. The Don Giovanni lamp by the Iranian-Egyptian architect and designer India Mahdavi completes the symphony in pastels. A cubbyhole filled with items that are as useful as they are charming emphasizes the intimacy of the place.

KIDS' KINGDOM

The children have their own seats, and the parents have theirs—with a chair or sofa for story time. Powder-pink and white suggest a cocoon-like warmth, perfect for tender moments. Off-limits at the moment for the smaller children, the shelf that runs along the wall is ready to welcome their future souvenir collection. Children need space to thrive and an attractive environment to stimulate their choices in the future. It's a room that should not be neglected!

GET THE LOOK

Fig. 1

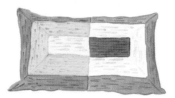

Heaps of cushions create their
own effects according
to the mood in the room.

Fig. 2

A rocking horse, a toy first
created in the Middle Ages
and revered in the eighteenth
century, adds a poetic touch.

Fig. 3

A wicker basket—Sézane's
summer "It" bag—is also
great for storage.

Fig. 4

These candles by Astier
de Villatte, the most Parisian
of brands, sums up the spirit
of Saint-Germain-des-Prés.

Fig. 5

Create a stack of boxes to hold
cosmetics or anything you
want to hide away.

Fig. 6

Metal trunks—army
footlockers—look good
anywhere and make
perfect shelves.

Fig. 7

A simple coffee set can inspire
the choice of colors that
will create a harmonious
and warm interior.

Fig. 8

In vogue during
the early twentieth century,
the Hawaiian ukulele is both
a toy and a beautiful object.

Fig. 9

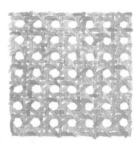

Whether vintage or modern,
rattan (from the stem of a
Southeast Asian shrub) puts
everyone in the vacation mood.

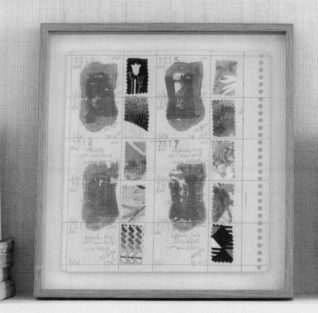

ALBERT COHEN

BELLE
DU SEIGNEUR

roman

nrf

GALLIMARD

*Partons, dans un baiser,
pour un monde inconnu.*

Alfred de Musset

Pastel

"Objects that we find at flea markets—and that we love—provide us with inspiration. It might start with the colors in a photo or a Persian rug, and gradually everything coalesces around this, very organically. I love that—the feeling that nothing is planned but everything is connected."

BRIMSTONE BUTTERFLY

ADONIS BLUE BUTTERFLY

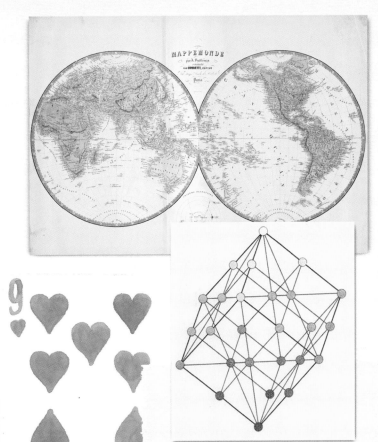

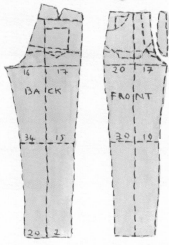

"Our apartment is made up of organic compositions. I like the way 'tableaux' emerge—it's nice to look at and triggers memories."

The
Nettle Butterfly
The caterpillar of this elegant butterfly feeds principally on thistles and nettles. It changes into a chrysalis in July, and the fly appears in August.
M. P. 1834.

Music- Guitar

Chez Anne & Georg

Sharing the same creative spirit, painter Georg Hallensleben and writer Anne Gutman, authors of children's stories, have turned their urban apartment into a veritable country house.

Pleasantly located on a very quiet street in the "village" of Saint-Paul, this home lies a stone's throw from the banks of the Seine and the Île Saint-Louis. Formerly the parish of the kings of France, the Marais district is filled with leafy courtyards and oases of greenery hidden behind closed doors. The seven rooms of this 1,722-square-foot (160 m²) apartment, arranged in a horseshoe shape, feature large French windows opening onto a tranquil terrace. With bedrooms on an upper level, this quirky space immediately charmed the two artists, whose crazy tales about the characters Penelope, Gaspard, and Lisa enthrall small children. For their own three children and their cat, they have never wanted to "decorate just for the sake of it," preferring to be led by their hearts and their imaginations. A movie buff, Anne drew inspiration from her favorite on-screen interiors to fill their home with a welcoming and authentic bucolic charm.

The fireplace, the old doors, and the cupboards attached to the walls feature among the treasures they have salvaged and refurbished. One fascinating historical detail: the kitchen floor was renovated using cement tiles, exhibited for the first time at the 1867 Paris World's Fair.

Georg and Anne have two weaknesses: the combination of stone and wood, and the happy blend of white, gray, and linen colors. And they dream of acquiring a drawing by Bonnard or a painting by Cy Twombly.

№ 122

At Home with History

A devotee of seventeenth-century interiors and 1950s chairs, Anne marries the two in a combination of styles and eras. But it is the kitchen— rustic down to the last detail—that sets the tone for the whole apartment. Rush-seated dining chairs surround the table, cotton curtains hang beneath the countertop, a former butcher's sideboard freshly painted in gray is home to assorted supplies, and a zinc bottle rack accommodates the glasses. Everything is vintage, even the colorful kitchen brushes displayed in an old glass jar.

LOSE TRACK OF TIME

The Louis-Philippe dresser, with its distressed white
finish, is filled with paperwork filed in Muji binders
and a collection of transparent glass canisters. The April
Vase by Tsé & Tsé on the ledge of the dresser provides
a modern accent, while a Tolomeo reading lamp
by Michele De Lucchi spotlights an old patched-up
rattan garden chair to create a theatrical setting.
Nearby, iconic Liberty-print cardboard suitcases
are stacked on a wicker hamper.

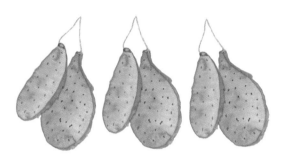

HARMONIES IN GREEN

Arrange flowers in a water jug, grow herbs in a candle votive, and why not dry cactus leaves on a section of stainless-steel railing? Go online to find banks of drawers once used in stores or workshops—they make perfect partitions for dividing up a room. Play with proportions by hanging a gigantic industrial-style clock next to a convex mirror that contains infinite reflections, and perch a collection of small china and glassware items on the mantel.

THE DEVIL'S IN THE DETAIL

There are as many readers as there are bookshelf styles.
Art book lovers go for shelves with plenty of height,
while novels can fit on smaller shelves, here at the
bottom of the bookcase. A wrought-iron child's bed
need not be consigned to the attic: it makes an ideal
chaise longue, adorned with pillows and cushions.
The old school desk looks completely at home alongside
a Harry Bertoia chair. The sense of harmony extends
to the color of the spirals on the notebooks,
which perfectly match the cactus.

PORCELAIN PERFECTION

Marco Polo discovered porcelain in China, and the delicate, translucent ceramic can bring a retro look to finger plates around plugs and switches—an important detail if you're going for a quaint interior. Another soft, flattering material is marble, whose look and easy maintenance make it a desirable alternative to tiling. Neutral tones in the bathroom don't compete with the colorful toiletries, and the wood of the door— buffed to a soft sheen—beautifully complements the shades of gray.

A WASHBASIN MADE FOR TWO

Above a classic double washbasin, two faucets
accommodate a shared washroom moment.
Wicker baskets, boxes, and crates can be stored
conveniently under the sink, while a wooden shelf
above has been simply painted to match the wall color.
Vintage mirrors just need a lick of paint to become
a pretty, reflective backdrop for perfume bottles or
soothing succulents. A workshop storage rack is much
more fun for children than a chest, and they'll love
arranging and rearranging their toys in the pigeonholes.

GET THE LOOK

Fig. 1

Don't throw out balsawood vegetable baskets: they make perfect containers for all of your little trinkets.

Fig. 2

Salvaged from a tailoring or upholstery workshop, these spools of thread are decorative objects in themselves.

Fig. 3

Keep old orange crates: they're a great size, colorful, and really useful—and they lend a touch of poetry.

Fig. 4

Line a whole wall with beautiful books to bring color and enjoyment to a room, but don't forget the stepladder.

Fig. 5

An essential feature in a retro interior, a rise-and-fall pendant lamp casts a pretty glow over the table.

Fig. 6

Whether old-fashioned hand-blown or contemporary glass, cloches make a feature of plants and precious objects alike.

Fig. 7

Unearthed at the flea market, given as presents, upcycled, or avidly collected, these little bowls make an impact in the kitchen or china cabinet.

Fig. 8

Dreaming of far-flung places? Maps rival pictures for decorative effect.

Fig. 9

Artists carefully hang on to their paint palettes, but bargain hunters can track them down at flea markets to use as decorative objects.

"It's hard to say what lends a Parisian touch to our apartment, because people often tell us that they don't feel as if they're in Paris here."

"Our favorite colors are white, gray, and linen— for its softness."

FLEURS ANCIENNES

(Reproductions d'après les Peintures du temps)
3ᵉ Série

Albert GARCET
EDITEUR

3, Rue Léon-Bosquai, PARC-ST-MAUR (Seine)

LINUM TENUIFOLIUM

"People say that our
apartment feels
like a house
in the country."

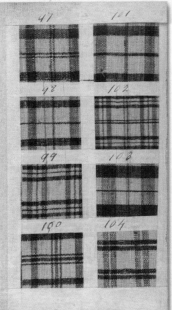

6309. GIANT CACTUS, ARIZONA.

OFFICINA PROFUMO FARMACEUTICA

FONDATA   NEL 1612

DI SANTA MARIA NOVELLA

FIRENZE

SAPONE PER UOMO

Chez Clémentine

BUTTES CHAUMONT DISTRICT
- PARIS 19ᵉ -

Like an idyllic sunset over the Atlantic or the Mediterranean, Clémentine Sarramon suffuses her apartment near the Parc des Buttes Chaumont with a vacation spirit. The interior designer finesses its proportions to create the illusion of space in just 516 square feet (48 m²).

The light-filled rooms in this double-sided apartment—with views of the Butte Bergeyre hilltop gardens on one side and the plane trees of Avenue Bolivar on the other—encourage the sense of being faraway, nurtured by Clémentine's trips to Africa and South America, and by the colorful atmosphere of her neighborhood. While favoring a minimalist style of clean lines in her professional projects, at home she has let her imagination run wild, designing an extremely cozy space with multiple nooks and corners filled with storied treasures.

Following her heart, Clémentine Sarramon has replicated the warm atmosphere of her family home in southwest France and the infectious charm of her native region using elements typical of the Basque Country or nearby Spain. Aiming for perfection, Clémentine sanded the 1930s floor to achieve a raw look that reveals the warm, golden hues of the wood. Her use of white showcases the apartment's art deco details, while powdery pigments make them glow, and China blue turns the bedroom into a self-contained cocoon. As a food and wine lover, Clémentine has organized her kitchen like a paean to good taste and indulgence, leaving all the utensils on display.

NOOKS AND CRANNIES

Positioning a chaise longue and a modern sofa opposite
each other directs traffic through the room and,
above all, turns it into a convivial space. In front of
the window, the AA (or Butterfly) armchair created
by designers Kurchan, Ferrari-Hardoy, and Bonet in
1938 is a classic choice in a beautiful setting, reflected
in the Venetian mirror in the corridor. The living room
appears spacious because it is made up of several corners
devoted to writing, reading, or eating. The wooden
features provide fragrance, warmth,
and softness.

A FEAST FOR THE EYES

A Louis-Philippe-era chaise longue with bolster,
upholstered in a sensual gold velvet, hosts a row
of cushions in varied fabrics and laid-back colors—
a master class in updating a vintage piece of furniture.
As a means of self-expression and self-fulfillment,
designing interior spaces is a great remedy for boredom
and introspection. You can have fun every day creating
vivid still lifes, then rearrange them according to your
mood or your latest find—it's visually very satisfying
and a great way to unwind.

ENHANCE YOUR ENTRANCE

More than just a passageway where you kick off your
shoes and hang your coat on a hook, the hallway
is a room in itself. A hallstand with drawers avoids
the need for cluttered coin trays and provides
a showcase for trinkets or souvenirs, such as seashells
collected on the shore or a globe to inspire a life
of travel. The octagonal Venetian mirror reflects
the living room and a view over the trees: it's a way
of opening up the closed space to the outside world
and bringing in natural light.

JEWEL IN THE CROWN

The bedroom is modest in size and has been conceived
as a jewel box, with dark blue on two walls and skirting,
plus matching furniture to blend in. This gives the space
depth and makes it seem bigger. The rough, wooden
bedside table and the yellow shell of the chair subtly
emphasize the blue. To create curtains, two lengths
of ikat fabric acquired abroad have been simply clipped
on to the rod so that the material can be changed
as often as desired; sweet dreams are guaranteed.

TAKE SPACE SERIOUSLY

Placed simply against the wall, the bed consists of a box
spring and a mattress. Linen sheets and ethnic fabrics
provide subtle coverings. Thanks to its delicate shape
and small proportions, a 1950s Scandinavian desk sits
easily against the narrow wall, and its weightless form
doesn't overload the space. Just two photo mementoes
are hung from colored string against the dark blue
wall to avoid disrupting the feeling of depth;
a watercolor mirrors them discreetly
with its pastel tones.

SMART STORAGE

An old chest of drawers is the perfect storage solution
for all sorts of things. Give it a fresh look using
a matte red paint that enhances its marble top
and blends with the dark blue. A wax-print cushion
on the rattan chair recalls the harmonious trio of colors
including the yellow of a coat peg, hidden behind
the door and useful for hanging up bags. Porcelain
door handles from old apartments are a feature worth
preserving for their character and tactile quality.
Leather straps make opening the closet easy.

A Matter of Taste

A wooden shelf above and an ethnic-patterned curtain below conceal the washing machine. Handmade Moroccan *zellige* tiles create a multicolored checkerboard on the wall. Their taupe, brick, and gray hues harmonize with the elegant gray-green backdrop, which also features on the tiny 1950s medicine cabinet and is highlighted by a coat hook in soft pink. The stage is set for paintings, convex mirrors, wicker baskets, and ceramics, while bracelets are stacked to form a kaleidoscopic sculpture.

SHOW AND TELL

An oasis of good living and indulgence, the kitchen is as appetizing as the dishes that are prepared in it. Everything is close at hand, and the smallest can becomes a collector's item. A shelf above the backsplash holds a collection of glasses and crockery. The white ceramic sink boasts a similarly neutral faucet so that only the utensils around it are visible. Old *azulejo* tiles, sourced in Portugal, lean up against the Paris subway-style tiling to strike an ornamental note.

GET THE LOOK

Fig. 1

A bamboo and ostrich-feather duster is a must-have item for the serious collector!

Fig. 2

Highly sought after, genuine Basque-style pottery is made in Sarreguemines, a town in the Moselle region that has specialized in ceramics since 1790.

Fig. 3

This glass jar is home to a little bit of nature that needs watering only once a year—a boon for those who don't have green thumbs!

Fig. 4

Antique linen brings relaxed and timeless elegance to cushion covers and bedspreads.

Fig. 5

Whether it's 1940s or older, you can make the most of a stylish and roomy chest of drawers by updating it.

Fig. 6

Manufactured only in Spain, these wood-handled knives are unbeatable for slicing *pata negra* ham.

Fig. 7

Something for armchair travelers: the globe, a familiar presence in 1970s children's bedrooms, can be unearthed at garage sales or antiques markets.

Fig. 8

Plastic "scoubidou" wine-bottle holders like this one were popular during the 1960s; look out for them today online.

Fig. 9

Iconoclastic Italian designer Paola Navone drew inspiration from the 1930s to create this fish-shaped bottle.

"I love creating harmonies between colors and materials— as much as I adore objects and fabrics with bold patterns!"

OGDEN'S CIGARETTES

T. 7. Nº 31.

CITRUS.

ÉTOFFES ET TAPIS ÉTRANGERS

Fig. 447. Oursin (1).

225

"My inspiration for decorating my apartment comes from my family home in the southwest and from my travels throughout the world."

T. 7. N° 33.

Fig. 1

Fig. 3.

CITRUS Aurantium.

P. Bessa pinx.

BRITISH SHELLS PL. IX.

G. B. Sowerby.

Aux Buttes Chaumont

Chapeau Paille Canotier
1F45 & 3F50

Chapeau Feutre Souple
3F50 & 6F50

Chapeau Paille Enfant
1F45 & 5F90

BOULEVARD DE LA VILLETTE A L'ANGLE DU FAUBOURG SAINT MARTIN

Chez Anthony & Benoît

The trio behind Atelier Vime are wholeheartedly devoted
to the basketwork that they jointly reinvent through their innovative
creations. Their name derives from an abbreviation of the Latin for the
willow used in basket weaving, *Salix viminalis*, and their visual world
is intimately related to eighteenth-century Provence.

Their workspace occupies several rooms in a 1,937-square-foot
(180 m^2), two-story apartment, where Anthony and Benoît have also
set up home. From this seventh-arrondissement building, they can hear
morning birdsong, and they never tire of the view across the rooftops or,
in the summer, the sunsets over the Eiffel Tower and the Musée d'Orsay.
Purveyors of a lifestyle featuring rattan, wicker, and rope, handcrafted
by artisans in the Camargue, they also collect vintage pieces
by Jean Royère, Gio Ponti, and Audoux & Minet. Their eclectic tastes
are influenced by their passion for these rustic materials, which provide
a natural contrast to the urban environment. Mixing eras and genres,
they focus mainly on balance, creating a coherence between form
and content; for example, they preserved the Haussmann-era fireplaces
but repainted them. Harmony is created through the use of perfect
proportions: the Tulip coffee table by Eero Saarinen for Knoll is
surrounded by low rope chairs by Adrien Audoux and Frida Minet.
While they are particularly fond of blue, green, and yellow, they are also
perfectly happy to choose brick red as the color for a built-in bookcase,
or to mix up printed fabrics and multicolored carpets. In fact, their dream
acquisition would be a Paule Leleu carpet, produced by Alexia Leleu.

MATERIAL MATTERS

Mixing genres also means daring to combine
materials without fear or favor. Rope, wood, marble,
and cast aluminum create a natural harmony.
The Eero Saarinen Tulip table chimes perfectly
with the Audoux & Minet rope chair and a brilliant-
yellow coffee set. Transforming flea-market finds
adds another layer of originality. The stained-glass
fanlight, of a type usually found above a door, proves
a perfect fit within the frame of the mirror hanging
over the marble fireplace.

CARPET BOMBING

Whether vintage, modern, or reissued classics, carpets create a warm atmosphere and protect wooden floors from cracks and scratches. Their colors can also have an impact on the choice of decor. One or more shades in a rug or carpet can find echoes in a cushion, a wall covering, or the window drapes. A tapestry wall hanging, while more delicate, makes a good substitute for a rug under a chair or side table; it is particularly effective for showcasing old or vintage designer furniture, such as the Audoux & Minet chair here.

RESPECT THE CLASSICS

Whether it's a Louis-XV-style cabriolet armchair
(it's no crime to add a lick of paint to the wood)
or a 1960s lounge chair by Geoffrey Harcourt, such
design classics work well in all settings—and the same
goes for fabrics. When reupholstering (on a budget)
a Directoire-style chaise longue, nothing can beat Toile
de Jouy. Produced from 1760 by Christophe-Philippe
Oberkampf in Jouy-en-Josas, ten miles southwest
of Paris and still the home of the eponymous museum,
Toile de Jouy is available in pink, blue,
gray, green, or black.

ELEGANT JUMBLE

Totally unique interiors can be created using small
assemblages of flea-market finds. The perfect place
can be found for everything, with a bit of daring.
An old Louis Vuitton monogrammed suitcase makes
ideal storage, particularly underneath the slant-top desk.
Overlooked corners provide a home for piles of books
and notebooks, while gouache paintings are propped
up informally on the floor. A *suzani*—an embroidered
textile from Central Asia—makes a delicate bedspread.

GET THE LOOK

Fig. 1

These 1940s rope-framed mirrors by Adrien Audoux and Frida Minet express a love of nature.

Fig. 2

Old chairs (not necessarily antiques) are still on-trend as well as being elegant and comfortable.

Fig. 3

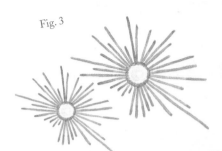

Different-sized constellation mirrors by Atelier Vime in natural rattan and wicker form an attractive wall grouping.

Fig. 4

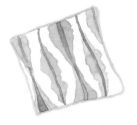

Add an ethnic touch with Pierre Frey cushions covered in ikat and tie-dye patterned linen.

Fig. 5

The Tulip chair, a twentieth-century design classic, was created by Finnish-American designer Eero Saarinen.

Fig. 6

An echo of the cabinet of curiosities Deyrolle in Paris: a stuffed bird mounted on a wooden plinth is an imaginative feature.

Fig. 7

The Edith lamp in natural wicker and black metal by Atelier Vime works well on a bedside table or by the fireplace.

Fig. 8

Nothing expresses a passion for the works of basket weavers like a vintage Audoux & Minet footstool.

Fig. 9

This carved-wood Provençal mirror, known as "de Beaucaire," has retained its original eighteenth-century gilding.

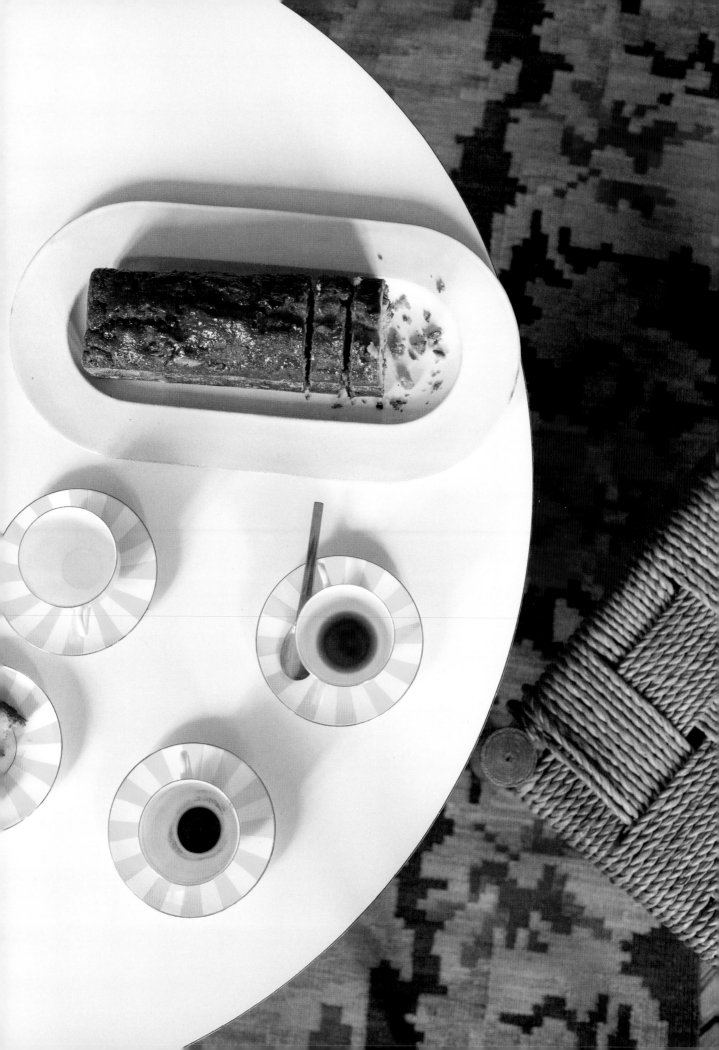

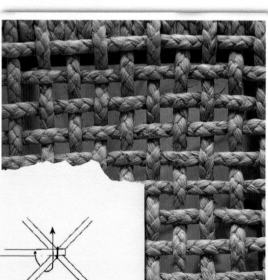

"Materials such as wicker, rattan, or rope offer a kind of natural counterpoint to the urban environment. It's a question of taste but also one of balance."

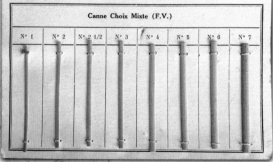

SOCIÉTÉ ANONYME DU ROTIN

26, Rue de Verdun, à CHAMPIGNY-sur-MARNE (Seine)

Canne Choix Mixte (F.V.)

N° 1	N° 2	N° 2 1/2	N° 3	N° 4	N° 5	N° 6	N° 7

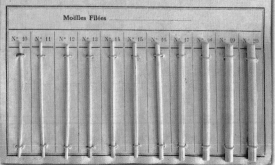

SOCIÉTÉ ANONYME DU ROTIN

26, Rue de Verdun, à CHAMPIGNY-sur-MARNE (Seine)

Moëlles Filées

N° 10	N° 11	N° 12	N° 13	N° 14	N° 15	N° 16	N° 17	N° 18	N° 19	N° 20

A 33762

№ 1

№ 2

№ 3

"The connection with Saint-Germain-
des-Prés is an emotional one. It's a daily
delight to cross the Pont du Carrousel
or the Passerelle des Arts bridges."

1115

A 8969+

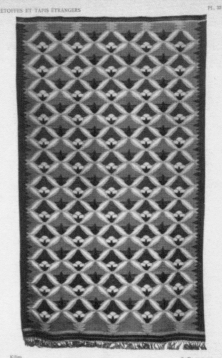

ÉTOFFES ET TAPIS ÉTRANGERS

Pl. 33

Kilim

E. Trojanowski
Industrie populaire, Varsovie.

6'A

PLACE
SAINT-GERMAIN
DES PRÉS

"Each era has produced
its own magnificent
spaces—there has to be
a coherence, a compatibility
between content and container."

FABRICATION
DE LA
VANNERIE
CANNAGE ET PAILLAGE
DES SIÈGES

Chez Louise

In Paris's artisan district, between Faubourg-Saint-Antoine and
Place de la Nation, Louise Jourdan-Gassin shares 516 square feet (48 m²)
of workshop-style space with her partner, Florent, and their dog, Ralph.
The founder of Série Limitée Louise—a brand of household linen
printed with vintage photos—Louise has lived in this former commercial
warehouse for ten years, enchanted by its location in a charming,
leafy private cul-de-sac, typical of the neighborhood.

Under the plasterwork, she was pleasantly surprised to discover a beautiful
brick-and-stone wall, which she has left on show to preserve the industrial
spirit of the place and create natural warmth. Rather than installing a new
floor that would have destroyed the vintage atmosphere, she was fortunate
enough to find a construction site where a pile of oak timbers had been
thrown into a dumpster. Once stripped, polished, and sawed to the right
dimensions, these timbers were used to create the wood flooring, which
looks as authentic as if it had always been there. In another recycling
project, beautiful old planks have been used to make the countertop,
the backsplash, and the shelf on the brick wall. The glass panel that
separates the bedroom from the bathroom was also uncovered
on a construction site.

As an expert in foraging for old photos at antique fairs and flea markets,
Louise has put her passion to good use when designing her home.
Avoiding the clichéd all-vintage look, she enjoys mixing up styles,
and the prevailing atmosphere gives you the impression of being
far from the hustle and bustle of Paris.

№ 170

BEAUTIFUL BRIC-À-BRAC

Overgrown with ivy, roses, and oleanders, the garden
adds a wild element that perfectly suits the overall
ambience. Caught between light and shadow,
the furniture and objects recall the mellow tones
of Flemish paintings. Set against the brick wall, a Tolix
Table 55 is used as a desk and frames the view outdoors.
Instead of an overly obtrusive ceiling light, the room
is illuminated in all four corners by hanging lamps
and table lamps.

WASTE NOT, WANT NOT

The worktop, backsplash, and shelf, cut from old
planks, bring an authentic touch by virtue of their
irregular shape and patina. Similarly, the old varnished
crate is used as a spice holder, with its contents neatly
stored in plastic bags and sealed with clothespins.
Old boxes, a cast-iron Staub cocotte, green tableware,
and books stacked against the backsplash add colorful
highlights. An upholsterer's table repainted in black
from Chehoma harmonizes with 1960s chairs
by Giancarlo Pieretti.

DIVE FOR PEARLS

Don't be afraid to pay a visit to construction sites
or to check out sidewalk treasures left for garbage
collection; you might find a rare gem, or an item
of furniture you may never have considered otherwise,
which will add a poetic touch to your interior with
its history and identity. One example is this side table,
still in its original shade of pale green, which hosts
a No. 207 lamp by Gras produced by DCW Éditions.
The bed linen complements this soft color,
underscored by a gray rug and stripped wooden posts.
The brushed-steel light switch provides one final,
industrial-style detail.

MIXED MEDIA

The bathroom, the final space in this mini loft apartment, appears larger thanks to the waxed concrete that extends from floor to ceiling. This material adds both simplicity and elegance through the richly nuanced shades it acquires once finished. Inspired by turn-of-the-century styles, both the washbasin and the freestanding bathtub create a classic, elegant look. A nineteenth-century mirror has been simply lime-washed to highlight its formerly gilded plasterwork. Privacy is ensured by a linen curtain in matching tones, which veils the courtyard window.

GET THE LOOK

Fig. 1

The wall-mounted rotating soap holder evokes memories of school days. The soap is usually lemon-shaped, a reminder for Louise of the perfumed lemon trees of Nice, her home town.

Fig. 2

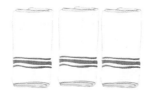

Louise collects washed-linen dish towels on which she prints black-and-white photos or the "Proust Questionnaire" personality test.

Fig. 3

The freestanding bathtub takes up less room than a modern bathtub and exudes an unrivaled sense of glamour.

Fig. 4

If you collect pretty vintage tableware, display it on a table or countertop.

Fig. 5

A pyramid-shaped pharmacy flask is perfect for catching the light, with its note of transparency, or for using as a vase.

Fig. 6

This bottle of orange blossom water by the Santa Maria Novella pharmacy in Florence makes a beautiful addition to the washbasin.

Fig. 7

Old wooden chopping boards are useful and make attractive decorative items.

Fig. 8

Look out for vintage light switches at flea markets—small details like these make all the difference when decorating an apartment.

Fig. 9

Filled with herbs or flour, or simply left empty, old glass storage jars are beautiful decorative objects.

"I live with the door open onto the garden, like a house, with my dog Ralph coming in and out all day long. It's really quite a timeless place, far from the hustle and bustle of the city."

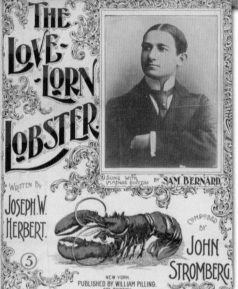

"In terms of style my apartment is a real mix—it's industrial and 1950s at the same time. I'm surrounded by objects that have already had a life and that have a story to tell."

Chez Marie-France

LES INVALIDES DISTRICT
- PARIS 7ᵉ -

The twentieth century boasts many iconic interior decorators and famous designers. However, the third millennium is epitomized by the whimsical moods of Marie-France Cohen, cofounder with her husband, Bernard Cohen, of the children's label Bonpoint and concept store Merci, and the creator of the Démodé brand. Following her intuition, Marie-France stumbled upon her ideal home: a house with a garden in the seventh arrondissement.

Inspired by her globe-trotting, early morning trawls through flea markets, voracious reading, and frequent museum visits, this iconoclast has created a timeless universe whose decor is the expression of her personality. She adores creating beautiful houses and seizes beauty wherever she finds it to create a space where memories of yesterday mingle with current passions. From minimalist to floral, from plain to baroque or 1930s, Marie-France plays around with conventional styles; she is not afraid to disregard fashions, even though fashion is an important part of her life. The soft light of the garden, the comfortable arrangement of rooms designed for living and entertaining, the aromas of toast and wood smoke, the beauty of colors and lovingly acquired paintings: these are the main characteristics of her home.

Lying somewhere between bohemian and sophisticated, each room reflects its owner: surprising, free, elegant, and unconventional. With the objects she has picked up—whether in China after falling in love, or from little market stalls around the world—Marie-France has created a decor that takes the roads less traveled by following her heart.

№184

VINTAGE CHARM

An old piece of furniture doesn't always need to be renovated: leave its patina and the marks of time and it will be all the more attractive. On the other hand, painting window- and door-frames black adds a little extra something. Juxtaposed with foliage, black makes all the greens stand out by accentuating the contrast. Galvanized iron pots, leaf-colored glassware, or a rust-spotted gueridon table all work well in the garden.

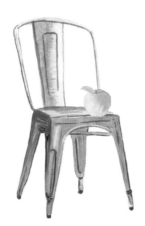

CULINARY PASSION

With its mix of rustic and industrial styles, the kitchen
has retained its original structure. Beneath a Semi
hanging lamp (by Fog & Morup, 1968), Tolix chairs
ring a tabletop balanced on the base of an old bistro
table. The black furniture and Ilve range stove contrast
vibrantly with the distressed tiling. A chest of drawers
is home to the table linen and cutlery. A mixture
of trinkets and crockery lines the shelves,
while potpourri nestles in a pair of scales.

ADDICTED TO BLACK

Black has many advantages. It helps create perspective, expresses intensity when paired with other colors, and creates a unique atmosphere. It perfectly offsets the Versailles parquet flooring and brings character to a fireplace, and black picture frames bring out the best in both oil paintings and drawings. A simple coat of matte black makes the rustic wooden table look totally different, complementing the gilded Louis XVI cane chairs. And painting is easy, even if you've never wielded a brush before.

COLLECTION PERFECTION

A piano stool next to the sideboard, a garden chair against a door, and a fireside armchair in its faded glory—seating is always attractive, and the more chairs you collect, the more your imagination will run wild. Babbitt metal statues are transformed into lamps; mirrors sit simply atop a piece of furniture; and pictures are hung close together, but never too high on the wall. Under the writing table, hatboxes are stored with casual charm.

CULTIVATE YOUR CURIOSITY

According to learned societies during
the Enlightenment, the creation of a cabinet
of curiosities should not be undertaken lightly.
Yet objects that appeal to the heart naturally seem
to create beautiful compositions. Here, a glass-fronted
black bookcase provides the perfect setting. Silverware,
shells, candlesticks, photographs, drawings, letters tied
with ribbon, bronzes, fragile vases, and other unusual
pieces form a natural collection. The two Renaissance
columns, a gift from Marie-France's husband
for their fiftieth wedding anniversary, fit into
the collection perfectly.

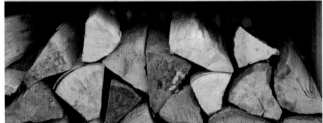

MAGIC CARPETS

Hand-tied in silk, cotton, or wool, Persian kilim
rugs are true works of art. Their graphic, floral,
or abstract designs blend perfectly with objects in every
style, including a soft-green cane banquette seat or a
twentieth-century design piece. The oldest kilims have
an enduring charm; they are exquisite even when worn,
their colors faded but still vivid. Several different carpets
from the same period can occupy the same space,
without ever offending the eye.

GET THE LOOK

Fig. 1

The first globes
appeared in the fifteenth
century, and since then they've
become an indispensable
decorative item.

Fig. 2

Chick and duckling taxidermy
mounts add childlike charm
to a cabinet of curiosities.

Fig. 3

Whether foraged at flea
markets or unearthed
in the attic, family portraits
(or those of smiling strangers!)
look great in pretty frames.

Fig. 4

Inspired by the process
of tin-plating mirrors,
candlesticks made of mercury
glass conjure up thoughts
of Bohemia and Moravia,
their countries of origin.

Fig. 5

A kaleidoscope of colored candles
makes an eye-catching feature
when set in candelabra
and candlesticks scattered
across the living-room table
or around the bathtub.

Fig. 6

Add a French touch with
a copy of *Un sang d'aquarelle* by
Françoise Sagan or Jeanne Galzy's
Pays perdu, published in Gallimard's
"La Blanche" collection of classic
French works, with crimson titles
on cream covers.

Fig. 7

"Without hesitation, I'd choose every
shade of green there is," says
Marie-France Cohen. In interior
design, a range of greens
is as important as the light
cast by many lamps.

Fig. 8

Once a vintage armchair has
been restuffed with horsehair,
there's no need to add new
upholstery: the thick white
canvas interfacing offers
timeless elegance.

Fig. 9

A gentle way to bring nature
into the home: countless bud
vases filled with flowers from
the garden or leaves from
the balcony.

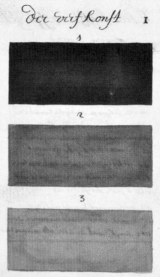

Der Verf Kunst 1

Der Verf Kunst 129

"My house is home to everything
I love—what's left of the past
and what I want today."

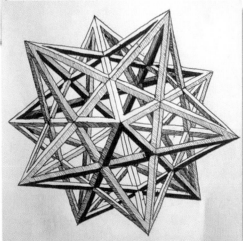

"In terms of taste, I allow myself
the right to disregard fashion,
even though, of course,
it's an important part of who I am.
I steal beauty wherever I find
it—I love houses with a passion."

FRANÇOISE SAGAN

Un sang
d'aquarelle

roman

nrf

GALLIMARD

Chez Margaux
& Rodolphe

BUTTES CHAUMONT DISTRICT
- PARIS 19ᵉ -

Like a Jacques Demy movie set starring Gene Kelly, pastel shades bring
a *Young Girls of Rochefort* feel to this apartment of 742 square feet (69 m²),
nestled in a 1930s building in Paris's nineteenth arrondissement.
Lawyer Margaux and screenwriter Rodolphe fell in love with its beautiful
rotunda, the balcony with its iron railings, the view of the Parc des Buttes
Chaumont, the art deco details, and the magical view of the skyline.

Delighted by how easy it is to move around the apartment and the perfect
proportions of each space, they have kept the glazed doors, which "act like
mental partitions." The arrival of their daughter, Madeleine, turned their
world Technicolor—pink, pale green, and sky blue. It's a gentle way of life
that they share in a sleek, classic, poetic style. Without removing any
of the 1930s features—oak flooring, moldings, or mirrors—they have
turned the kitchen into a bedroom, relocating the kitchen to
the double living room. The only remnant of this transformation
is the original terrazzo kitchen floor, now underfoot in Madeleine's
bedroom. Fashionable between the wars and originating in Italy, this
composite flooring made of marble and glass chips is once again back
in vogue. The 3D effect of the floor's polished surface blends happily with
the pale woodwork and soft colors chosen by Margaux and Rodolphe.
To offset the apartment's formal character, they have created a timeless
charm using vintage furniture and objects, contemporary Scandinavian
furniture, and idyllic design pieces, such as the Cap d'Ail
side table by Mathieu Matégot.

№ 202

MIX AND MATCH

Opposite the window, the Napoleon III-era chaise longue, a family heirloom, has been upholstered in pale linen for a more contemporary look. On the modern sofa, a French blue throw echoes the same color in the painting propped up on the floor. The marriage globes, usually found empty at flea markets, are used to display favorite collections. To make it look bigger, the office is filled to the rafters. In cozy 1950s style, the low cabinet doubles as both a bookcase and seat. A leather plumber's bag is ideal for storing bits and bobs or tools.

BABY'S REALM

While the walls sport pastel tones, the ceiling and door are painted in a downy white (Wimborne White by Farrow & Ball), which is used throughout the apartment for its velvety warmth. The wardrobe stretches the full height of the wall, blending in with the decor. To add a touch of delicacy to the chest of drawers, the wood has been stripped, leaving just the drawer handles painted white, while the mobile adds a splash of color.

EVERYTHING ON HAND

Designed as a single horizontal block floating off
the floor, the kitchen appears to be suspended in
space. Its pastel hue, white countertop, and knives
hanging from a magnetic holder on the backsplash
emphasize the light-as-air feeling. A long shelf
is all that's needed to hold everyday essentials,
ornamented with engravings and favorite objects.
While the owners' dream table (Nissen & Gehl's
Twist, produced by Naver) is on the wish list,
a white linen tablecloth elegantly camouflages
the current tabletop.

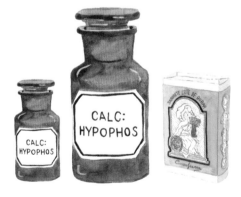

SOFT FOCUS

It took just a touch of powder-pink paint to turn
the bathroom into a luscious nest. The white
backdrop of tiles and woodwork makes the pink
stand out and creates volume. To give the impression
that the terrazzo flooring extends right up to the
wall, a mirror has been cleverly fitted onto the bath
panel. A rustic chair for clothes and apothecary jars
for cotton balls and rose water complete the picture.

GET THE LOOK

Fig. 1

Claus Porto soaps—made in Portugal and available online—have attractive art deco wrappers.

Fig. 2

Whether matching or not, coffee sets shouldn't be hidden away in a cupboard but put on display.

Fig. 3

Children's schoolbags—miniature in size, available in pretty colors, and embellished with prints—make charming decorative objects.

Fig. 4

For ultimate refinement, there are just two options when it comes to dishwashing liquid: hide it away or decant it into a striking flask.

Fig. 5

There's nothing wrong with loving food—and perfect pasta shapes make an attractive display when stored in glass jars.

Fig. 6

Collect pretty Spanish cans of Omega-3-rich crab or sardines—as much for the vintage design of their labels as for their taste!

Fig. 7

Instead of stashing your vacation mementoes in cardboard cases—like Brigitte Bardot in her song "La Madrague"—use glass domes to showcase your summer collection of seaside treasures.

Fig. 8

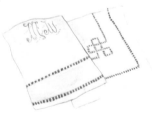

Steal your grandma's linen or track some down at flea markets. It'll look great after you boil it up to remove the starch.

Fig. 9

A vintage rocking chair, painted to match the nursery decor, is perfect for lulling baby to sleep or reading bedtime stories.

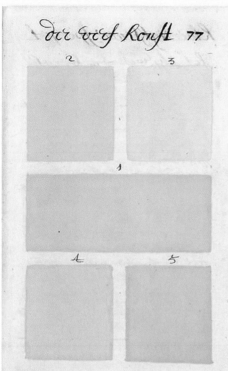

die verf konst 77

2   3

1

4   5

"Throughout the entire apartment we have chosen a warm white and pale pastel shades in blue-green or pink, allowing the light to prevail."

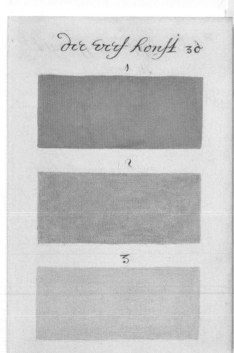

die verf konst 30

1

2

3

LA
BOTANIQUE
MISE
A LA PORTÉE DE TOUT LE MONDE
ou
COLLECTION
DES
PLANTES D'USAGE
DANS LA MEDECINE, DANS LES ALIMENS
ET DANS LES ARTS.

TOME 1.
A PARIS
MDCCLXXIV.

"Our trips to Argentina, Africa, and Asia are our primary source of inspiration."

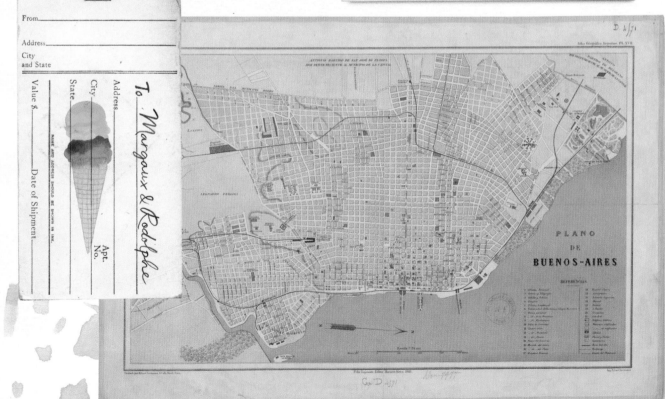

Chez Carole

In the heart of Saint-Germain-des-Prés, right next door
to the legendary Au Chai de l'Abbaye brasserie, the Salon gallery
is the go-to place for connoisseurs of French, Swedish,
and Italian antiques. And its founders, Carole and Stéphane
Borraz, also live on Paris's Left Bank.

A stone's throw from the Panthéon and facing the Luxembourg
Gardens, they and their two children occupy a Directoire-style
apartment, whose singular spaces exude an old-fashioned charm,
complete with indoor shutters and a marble fireplace that still
works in winter. Their renovation plan consisted of just a coat
of strategically applied paint—Provençal yellow for doors and
glass-fronted cupboards; gray-green for the bedroom, and white
everywhere else—to enhance their eclectic collections.
On shelves, mantelpieces, and in the cupboards, Carole displays
groups of antique sculptures: plaster casts that are unassuming,
graceful, and sensual. These are combined with an imaginative
theatricality that she adores—inspired by the interiors
at Villa Necchi Campiglio, the work of designers Studio
Peregalli in Milan, architect Carlo Mollino's home in Turin,
and the world of fashion designer Dries Van Noten. Stylistic
constraints are abandoned in this flight of imagination,
sensitivity, and bohemianism. In the decorative arts, like attracts
like—after which, anything goes. The impressive kitchen is filled
with astonishingly simple finds. All of these diverse items
reflect one aspiration: to create the good life—and that
is the secret of a successful interior.

Color Coordinated

Since the windows open onto
the treetops of the Luxembourg
Gardens, the use of green was
an obvious choice, bringing
nature indoors and
opening up the space.
Lit by a reading
lamp, two ostentatious
armchairs—a baroque
Italian design from the
1950s—play with surreal
proportions like a theater
set by Jean Cocteau. The wood
floor, the blue and gray of the
carpet, and finally the pink
and purple cushions chime
together with the green to
form a harmonious chromatic
circle, echoed by the pencil
holder on the desk.

HANGING COMMITTEE

When your desk is facing a wall, a decorative makeshift bulletin board brightens up the work day. Amid engravings and framed botanical studies, reminders and postcards are stuck to the wall using simple adhesive tape. Truly decorative elements, such as plaster busts or sculpture maquettes, can be found everywhere. The very monastic bedroom, with its carved raw-wood bedside table, recalls Arte Povera, the nomadic Italian art movement that began in 1967 as a challenge to industrialized society.

START A CABINET
OF CURIOSITIES

Creating your own miniature museum means sourcing
beautiful items, bringing together elements with
a shared origin, and choosing contrasting objects.
Sponges and corals fill a bowl atop a repainted stool,
while paintings, statuettes, and earthenware are
displayed along the fireplace mantel. A glass vitrine
is perfect for showing off rare finds. Cheval glass
dressing mirrors, hung in a group, evoke the spirit
of Renaissance cabinets of curiosities.

BRIGHTEN YOUR DAY

Functionality takes a back seat when creating a
dreamlike world that appeals to children and adults
alike. Hung above the bed, a swan made of sequins and
fabric (by New York artist Tamar Mogendorff) brings
the dream within reach. Rolls of antique wallpaper
offset the academic connotations of the blackboard.
A Formica kitchen chair comfortably replaces an overly
formal office chair. The Louis-Philippe-era pedestal
for a marriage globe is now home to an arrangement
of potted succulents.

SHOWCASE EVERYDAY ART

Whether acquired during your travels or on garage sale visits, vintage utensils adorn a kitchen perfectly. Alongside elegant cutting boards, a cat ornament, and Astier de Villatte tableware, the cast-iron Le Creuset casserole sits in a wooden basket— a promise of delicious dishes to come. Brushes and spoons provide the perfect accompaniment in this tribute to everyday art.

GET THE LOOK

Fig. 1

Collect multicolored pens and don't hide them away—they're part of the decor!

Fig. 2

A child's skateboard (often decorated by artists) is a design feature that can even serve as a showcase for a collection of objects.

Fig. 3

Full of the charms of yesteryear, antique apothecary bottles are highly collectible and work well as either vases or containers.

Fig. 4

Cushions by Lindell & Co. are handmade by Kashmiri artisans.

Fig. 5

Convex mirrors, also known as "witch mirrors" for the magical powers attributed to them, reflect the entire room.

Fig. 6

Select brushes that are as practical as they are pretty for a serious take on the domestic arts.

Fig. 7

This Diabolo lamp by Pierre Guariche from the 1950s is a treasured find that can be unearthed at flea markets.

Fig. 8

A plaster cast of a foot makes an ingenious arty doorstop.

Fig. 9

This pretty chest has been created using decorative sheets of paper or "dominos" by the three designers of À Paris Chez Antoinette Poisson.

"We made this apartment our own by injecting a good dose of color in certain strategic places."

"My favorite material is plaster—I love its sensuality, purity, delicacy, and theatricality."

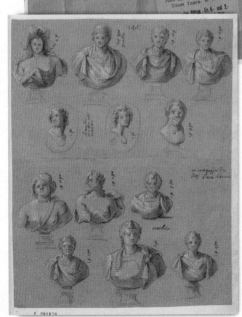

MOUVEMENT DADA

8. DADA-SOIREE

Saal zur Kaufleuten

9. April, abends 8¼ Uhr

Manifeste, Gedichte, Kompositionen, Tänze (5 Personen) und simultanistische Dichtungen (30 Personen).

Hans Arp, Viking Eggeling, Hans Heusser, Susanne Perrottet, Hans Richter, Walter Serner, Tristan Tzara, K. Wulff.

Eintritt Fr. 4.- und 2.-

Chez Sophie

If you want spectacular views of Paris, check out Leos Carax's movie *The Lovers on the Bridge*, or just gaze out of a window in the apartment of Sophie Duruflé, managing director of the Isabel Marant fashion label. From sunrise to sunset, views of the *bateaux-mouches* tourist boats on the Seine, the towers of the Conciergerie, and the Pont au Change bridge delight this incurable aesthete. One of Marant's childhood friends, Sophie divides her life between traveling, her daughter Héléna, her two cats, and her beautiful home.

White walls create a soothing atmosphere and, most importantly, lend themselves to all Sophie's decorative ideas. Throughout 2,260 square feet (210 m²) filled with moldings and exposed woodwork, her dreams run wild. Along recessed wall shelving, Sophie exhibits her collections of unglazed earthenware, glasses, apothecary jars, marriage globes, and vases, which she festoons with flowers. In each of the seven rooms, bouquets and plants intermingle everywhere, bringing a splash of color (white and green are Sophie's favorites). The scene pays tribute to nature, symbolized by the presence of birds and butterflies. Whether stuffed, ceramic, or framed, they represent a bucolic world that Sophie loves as a way of escaping the hustle and bustle of the city. Although she is a fan of the classic style, Sophie is not afraid to make her mark with inventions of her own, renovating old wooden furniture, stools with flaking paintwork, or ex-army cots.

Displaying her favorite things discovered by chance or foraged at flea markets, Sophie's quirky tastes shine through, illuminated at night by glimmering candlelight.

№ 234

NATURALLY POETIC

Antique pots on the balcony, exotic paintings, and stuffed
birds evoke travels to faraway places. The flamingo on a
sculptor's stool and the parrot perched on a branch were
acquired at Deyrolle, the Parisian taxidermy specialist.
On the *bergère* wing chair, draped with a sheepskin
throw, a tribal buffalo skull joins this cabinet
of life-size curiosities.

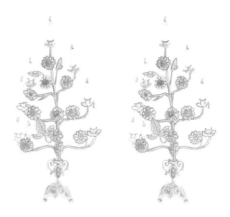

PRECIOUS TRANSPARENCY

Fabrics in general and linen in particular take center stage
in the simple transformation of an ordinary hanging lamp
wrapped in an old sheet. The feathery weightlessness
of a row of quill pens is reflected in the mirror.
Napoleon III-style bronze candlesticks and church
candelabra (often decorated with terra-cotta flowers,
known as biscuit ware) are lined up on the table.
Arranging similar objects in repeat patterns is one
of the golden rules of interior design.

FEMININITY TO THE FORE

Antique or Venetian mirrors, precious or costume jewelry,
Astier de Villatte ceramics—nothing is too luxurious for
a bedroom. Feminine touches can be felt everywhere here,
such as the novels wrapped in brown Kraft paper, their
titles handwritten by Sophie herself. Beneath the light
by Fleux, attached to a bird bought at Serendipity,
cushions by Caravan and by wallpaper designers Akin &
Suri mingle with treasures found in Brooklyn flea markets.

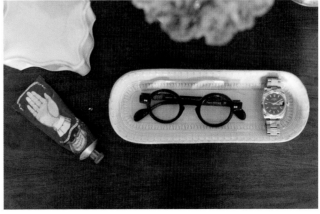

Take On the World

The whole world may now be within
everyone's reach in cyberspace,
but—in the world of interior
decoration—globes are
regaining territory.
Whether illuminated,
outsized, supported
by a bronze Atlas
(a nod to the Farnese
Atlas, a second-century
Roman sculpture), or set
on an aluminum or wooden
plinth, spherical maps are now
highly sought after by collectors,
as are marriage globes
housing sculpted columns
of seashells or flowers.
The patina of time does the rest.

CANDY COLORS

One way to make your kitchen as delicious as a box of candy is to decorate it in zesty colors, put everything on display, and set the table for occasions both big and small. Express your personal taste in the arrangement of glasses, canned foods, or choice of trash can. A cult object by Danish designer Holger Nielsen, the Pedal Bin was designed in 1939 for his wife's hair salon, proving that iconic design endures.

BATHING BEAUTIES

More often seen in kitchens, Parisian subway-style tiling here adorns the bathroom. Wooden crates house boxes covered in Liberty prints. A claw-foot bathtub, early twentieth-century sink, and old pharmacy jars add to the feeling of authenticity, alongside Savon de Marseille soaps. A filament bulb, with its gleaming light, can also be used to hang a collection of necklaces.

A BOUDOIR WITH BENEFITS

In the apartment's smallest room, Sophie has designed a blue boudoir "so I never feel lost at home." Insisting on smooth silk velvets and Indian check fabrics, she plays at *Princess and the Pea*, stacking several mattresses atop wooden pallets, and festooning the ceiling with festive paper lanterns brought back from China. While her favorite object is a paper sculpture by artist Georgia Russell, Sophie's cushion collection is a simple pleasure that can be copied inexpensively.

GET THE LOOK

Fig. 1

Barbers' mirrors allow you
to see yourself and your interior
in a flattering triptych. Whether
oval or rectangular, they work
well in small groups.

Fig. 2

Plates by Astier de Villatte come
in all designs: white, or printed
with images of animals, antique
statues, or colored checks.

Fig. 3

Charm your local construction
site manager or supermarket clerk
into giving you old wooden
pallets to make a base
for several mattresses.

Fig. 4

Hide the unattractive covers
of favorite books with Kraft paper,
and add a handwritten word that
describes each one perfectly.

Fig. 5

A beautiful example of lightness
and transparency, old chemistry-
class models of molecules can be
mounted on delicate plinths.

Fig. 6

Don't throw out old tea caddies—
they're ideal containers for tiny
plants, flowers, or herbs.

Fig. 7

Search army surplus stores
or flea markets for folding
army cots that, with a bit
of imagination, can make
wonderful sofas.

Fig. 8

Real treasures, these candle
holders by Officine Universelle
Buly serve as gorgeous storage
pots for pencils and pens.

Fig. 9

Collect design weekly
Cabana and arrange stacks
of back issues at the foot
of an armchair or sofa.

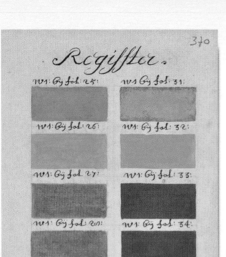

Register.

370

25 भारत INDIA

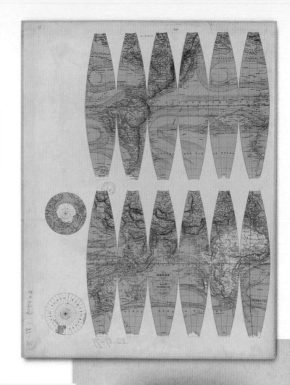

THE CHINESE PRIMROSE

SHORT-HAIRED BLUE

A LA FONTAINE DES PARFUMS

HUILE DE QUININE

SURFINE

LORENZY-PALANCA

PARFUMEUR MARSEILLE
PARIS - GRASSE

Pour l'entretien et la Régénération

"I collect and accumulate
lots of things,
but I'm trying
to declutter more
and more."

LARGE WHITE BUTTERFLY, LARVA & PUPA.

QUARTER ANNA

AIR INDIA INTERNATIONAL

FIRST FLIGHT 8TH JUNE 1948

INDIA POSTAGE 12 AS

"My favorite thing about this apartment is definitely the breathtaking view of the Seine river and the *bateaux-mouches* tourist boats!"

ART SUPPLIES

Magasin Sennelier
3 Quai Voltaire
75007 Paris
magasinsennelier.net

La Maison du Pastel
20 Rue Rambuteau
75003 Paris
lamaisondupastel.com

Relma
3 Rue Poitevins
75006 Paris
relma.fr

BEAUTY

Buly
6 Rue Bonaparte
75006 Paris
buly1803.com

Maison Claus Porto
135 Rua da Misericórdia
1200-272 Lisbon – Portugal
clausporto.com

Santa Maria Novella
16 Via della Scala
50123 Florence – Italy
smnovella.com

CONCEPT STORES

A Vida Portuguesa
11 Rua Anchieta
1200-023 Lisbon – Portugal
avidaportuguesa.com

Ines de la Fressange Paris
24 Rue de Grenelle
75007 Paris
inesdelafressange.fr

Merci
111 Boulevard Beaumarchais
75003 Paris
merci-merci.com

La Trésorerie
11 Rue du Château d'Eau
75010 Paris
latresorerie.fr

FABRICS

Larsen (showroom)
110 Fulham Road
London SW3 6HU – UK

Manuel Canovas (showroom)
6 Rue de l'Abbaye
75006 Paris
manuelcanovas.com

Pierre Frey (showroom)
27 Rue du Mail
75002 Paris

107 Design Centre East
Chelsea Harbour
London SW10 0XF – UK

pierrefrey.com

FLEA MARKETS AND ANTIQUE SHOPS

Broc'Martel
12 Rue Martel
75010 Paris
brocantelab.com/boutique/13966

L'Objet Qui Parle
86 Rue des Martyrs
75018 Paris

Portobello Paris
56 Rue Notre Dame des Champs
75006 Paris
portobello-paris.com

Puces de Saint-Ouen, Marché Paul Bert
18 Rue Paul Bert
93400 Saint-Ouen
paulbert-serpette.com/le-marche

Puces de Vanves
Avenue Marc Sangnier, 75014 Paris
Avenue Georges Lafenestre, 75014 Paris
pucesdevanves.fr

Trolls et Puces/Belle Lurette
1 & 5 Rue du Marché Popincourt
75011 Paris
brocantes-popincourt.com

Yveline Antiques
4 Rue de Furstemberg
75006 Paris
yveline-antiquites.com

FLORISTS

Arôm
73 Avenue Ledru-Rollin
75012 Paris
aromparis.fr

Bergamotte
bergamotte.com

Thalie
223 Rue Saint-Jacques
75005 Paris

INTERIORS AND HOME ACCESSORIES

Ailleurs
17 Rue Saint-Nicolas
75012 Paris
ailleurs-paris.com

Alix D. Reynis
14 Rue Commines
75003 Paris
alixdreynis.com

Antoinette Poisson
12 Rue Saint-Sabin
75011 Paris
antoinettepoisson.com

Astier de Villatte
173 Rue Saint Honoré
75001 Paris
astierdevillatte.com

Atelier Vime
ateliervime.com

Bazar d'Électricité
34 Boulevard Henri IV
75004 Paris
bazarelec.com

Le Bon Marché
24 Rue de Sèvres
75007 Paris
24sevres.com

Caravane
19 & 22 Rue Saint-Nicolas
75012 Paris
caravane.fr

Cire Trudon
78 Rue de Seine
75006 Paris

36 Chiltern Street
London W1U 7QJ - UK

248 Elizabeth Street
New York, NY 10012 - US

2F Starfield Hanam, 750
Misa-daero
Hanam-si - South Korea
trudon.com

Démodé
70 Rue de Grenelle
75007 Paris
demode.fr

Deyrolle
46 Rue du Bac
75007 Paris
deyrolle.com

Diptyque
34 Boulevard Saint-Germain
75005 Paris
diptypeparis.fr

Emery & Cie
18 Passage de la Main d'Or
75011 Paris
emeryetcie.com

Jamini
10 Rue du Château d'Eau
75010 Paris
jaminidesign.com/en

Jieldé
jielde.com

Khadi and Co.
82 Boulevard Beaumarchais
75011 Paris
maison-objet.com/en/paris/
exhibitors/january-2018/
khadi-and-co

Liberty London
Regent Street
London W1B 5AH - UK
libertylondon.com

Maison Aimable
16-18 Rue des Taillandiers
75011 Paris
maison-aimable.com

Maison Leleu
86 Rue Lemercier
75017 Paris
maisonleleu.com

Ressource
2-4 Avenue du Maine
75015 Paris
ressource-peintures.com

Tensira
21 Place des Vosges
75003 Paris
tensira.com

TOYS AND ACCESSORIES FOR KIDS

Bass et Bass
229 Rue Saint-Jacques
75005 Paris
bassetbass.fr

Petit Pan
36 Rue des Abbesses
75018 Paris
petitpan.com

ONLINE STORES

artnet.com

bergamotte.com

brocantelab.com

conranshop.co.uk

design-market.fr

inesdelafressange.fr

marinmontagut.com

INES THANKS

my editors, who are crazy, for always being enthusiastic about all my projects
and providing trust and absolute freedom (and, um, a sense of humor);

-

Françoise Dorget, Marie-France Cohen, Jacques Grange,
and Madeleine Castaing, who for me have always been
masters in the art of decoration;

-

Toto (aka Vincent Vanechop), because it's not enough to find great furniture,
you also need a good mover! (vincent.vanechop@wanadoo.fr);

-

Sophie Gachet, because when, for once, I did a book without her,
she didn't even have a jealous fit;

-

Marin, who knows me so well that there are many things
I don't even have to do;

-

Denis, who lets me decorate the house however I want and
finds it totally normal that my closet is bigger than his;

-

the kind bookseller who displays this book so well and considers
it the best interiors book of the decade;

-

Dinky and Mosca, who think I've done such a good job of choosing
the sofas that they tend to cover them in dog fur;

-

Simon, if you stop hosing down the entire bathroom
every time you take a shower!

-

And, finally, thanks to my readers, who don't like "showroom" houses
or "fashion victims," but who remain ever curious and on-trend.

MARIN THANKS

all of the families who opened their doors to us with a smile;

-

my *maman* for passing on to me a taste for beautiful things;

-

my sister for her precious advice;

-

Ines for her friendship;

-

and my editors Kate and Julie for their trust in me.

GAMMES DE COULEURS

№ 0 0 0 1

№ 0 0 0 2

№ 0 0 0 3

№ 0 0 0 4

№ 0 0 0 5

№ 0 0 0 6

№ 0 0 0 7

№ 0 0 0 8

№ 0 0 0 9

№ 0 0 1 0

№ 0 0 1 1

№ 0 0 1 2

SOUS LES TOITS DE PARIS

№ 0013

№ 0014

№ 0015

№ 0016

№ 0017

№ 0018

№ 0019

№ 0020

№ 0021

№ 0022

№ 0023

№ 0024

I & M